This planner belongs to:

Twenty-one

January

S	M	T	W	T	F	S
					1	2
3	4	5	6	7	8	9
10	11	12	13	14	15	16
17	18	19	20	21	22	23
24	25	26	27	28	29	30
31						

February

S	M	T	W	T	F	S
	1	2	3	4	5	6
7	8	9	10	11	12	13
14	15	16	17	18	19	20
21	22	23	24	25	26	27
28						

March

S	M	T	W	T	F	S
	1	2	3	4	5	6
7	8	9	10	11	12	13
14	15	16	17	18	19	20
21	22	23	24	25	26	27
28	29	30	31			

April

S	M	T	W	T	F	S
				1	2	3
4	5	6	7	8	9	10
11	12	13	14	15	16	17
18	19	20	21	22	23	24
25	26	27	28	29	30	

May

S	M	T	W	T	F	S
						1
2	3	4	5	6	7	8
9	10	11	12	13	14	15
16	17	18	19	20	21	22
23	24	25	26	27	28	29
30	31					

June

S	M	T	W	T	F	S
		1	2	3	4	5
6	7	8	9	10	11	12
13	14	15	16	17	18	19
20	21	22	23	24	25	26
27	28	29	30			

July

S	M	T	W	T	F	S
				1	2	3
4	5	6	7	8	9	10
11	12	13	14	15	16	17
18	19	20	21	22	23	24
25	26	27	28	29	30	31

August

S	M	T	W	T	F	S
1	2	3	4	5	6	7
8	9	10	11	12	13	14
15	16	17	18	19	20	21
22	23	24	25	26	27	28
29	30	31				

September

S	M	T	W	T	F	S
			1	2	3	4
5	6	7	8	9	10	11
12	13	14	15	16	17	18
19	20	21	22	23	24	25
26	27	28	29	30		

October

S	M	T	W	T	F	S
					1	2
3	4	5	6	7	8	9
10	11	12	13	14	15	16
17	18	19	20	21	22	23
24	25	26	27	28	29	30
31						

November

S	M	T	W	T	F	S
	1	2	3	4	5	6
7	8	9	10	11	12	13
14	15	16	17	18	19	20
21	22	23	24	25	26	27
28	29	30				

December

S	M	T	W	T	F	S
			1	2	3	4
5	6	7	8	9	10	11
12	13	14	15	16	17	18
19	20	21	22	23	24	25
26	27	28	29	30	31	

Year in Pixels

	J	F	M	A	M	J	J	A	S	O	N	D
1.												
2.												
3.												
4.												
5.												
6.												
7.												
8.												
9.												
10.												
11.												
12.												
13.												
14.												
15.												
16.												
17.												
18.												
19.												
20.												
21.												
22.												
23.												
24.												
25.												
26.												
27.												
28.												
29.												
30.												
31.												

Color Codes

Notes

January

2021

SUNDAY	MONDAY	TUESDAY	WEDNESDAY
3	4	5	6
10	11	12	13
17	18	19	20
24	25	26	27

January

2021

THURSDAY	FRIDAY	SATURDAY	NOTES
	1	2	
7	8	9	
14	15	16	
21	22	23	
28	29	30	31

February 2021

SUNDAY	MONDAY	TUESDAY	WEDNESDAY
	1	2	3
7	8	9	10
14	15	16	17
21	22	23	24
28			

February 2021

THURSDAY	FRIDAY	SATURDAY	NOTES
4	5	6	
11	12	13	
18	19	20	
25	26	27	
			NOTES

March 2021

SUNDAY	MONDAY	TUESDAY	WEDNESDAY
	1	2	3
7	8	9	10
14	15	16	17
21	22	23	24
28	29	30	31

March

2021

THURSDAY	FRIDAY	SATURDAY	NOTES
4	5	6	
11	12	13	
18	19	20	
25	26	27	
			NOTES

April 2021

SUNDAY	MONDAY	TUESDAY	WEDNESDAY
4	5	6	7
11	12	13	14
18	19	20	21
25	26	27	28

April

2021

THURSDAY	FRIDAY	SATURDAY	NOTES
1	2	3	
8	9	10	
15	16	17	
22	23	24	
29	30	1	NOTES

May 2021

SUNDAY	MONDAY	TUESDAY	WEDNESDAY
2	3	4	5
9	10	11	12
16	17	18	19
23	24	25	26
30	31		

May

2021

THURSDAY	FRIDAY	SATURDAY	NOTES
6	7	8	
13	14	15	
20	21	22	
27	28	29	
			NOTES

June 2021

SUNDAY	MONDAY	TUESDAY	WEDNESDAY
		1	2
6	7	8	9
13	14	15	16
20	21	22	23
27	28	29	30

June

2021

THURSDAY	FRIDAY	SATURDAY	NOTES
3	4	5	
10	11	12	
17	18	19	
24	25	26	
			NOTES

July

2021

SUNDAY	MONDAY	TUESDAY	WEDNESDAY
4	5	6	7
11	12	13	14
18	19	20	21
25	26	27	28

July

2021

THURSDAY	FRIDAY	SATURDAY	NOTES
1	2	3	
8	9	10	
15	16	17	
22	23	24	
29	30	31	NOTES

August

2021

SUNDAY	MONDAY	TUESDAY	WEDNESDAY
1	2	3	4
8	9	10	11
15	16	17	18
22	23	24	25
29	30	31	

August

2021

THURSDAY	FRIDAY	SATURDAY	NOTES
5	6	7	
12	13	14	
19	20	21	
26	27	28	NOTES

September 2021

SUNDAY	MONDAY	TUESDAY	WEDNESDAY
			1
5	6	7	8
12	13	14	15
19	20	21	22
26	27	28	29

September

2021

THURSDAY	FRIDAY	SATURDAY	NOTES
2	3	4	
9	10	11	
16	17	18	
23	24	25	
30			NOTES

October 2021

SUNDAY	MONDAY	TUESDAY	WEDNESDAY
3	4	5	6
10	11	12	13
17	18	19	20
24	25	26	27

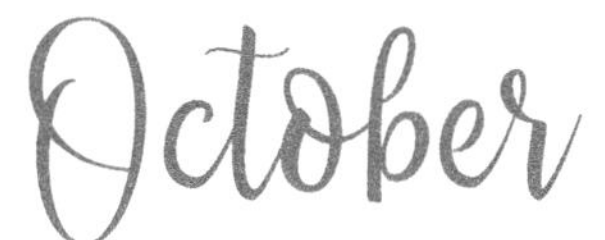

2021

THURSDAY	FRIDAY	SATURDAY	NOTES
	1	2	
7	8	9	
14	15	16	
21	22	23	
28	29	30 31 SUNDAY	NOTES

November 2021

SUNDAY	MONDAY	TUESDAY	WEDNESDAY
	1	2	3
7	8	9	10
14	15	16	17
21	22	23	24
28	29	30	

November

2021

THURSDAY	FRIDAY	SATURDAY	NOTES
4	5	6	
11	12	13	
18	19	20	
25	26	27	
			NOTES

December 2021

SUNDAY	MONDAY	TUESDAY	WEDNESDAY
			1
5	6	7	8
12	13	14	15
19	20	21	22
26	27	28	29

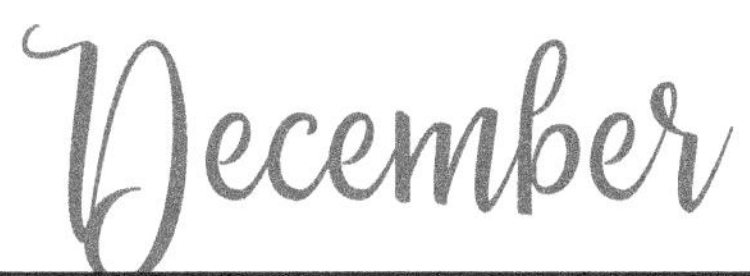

2021

THURSDAY	FRIDAY	SATURDAY	NOTES
2	3	4	
9	10	11	
16	17	18	
23	24	25	
30	31		NOTES

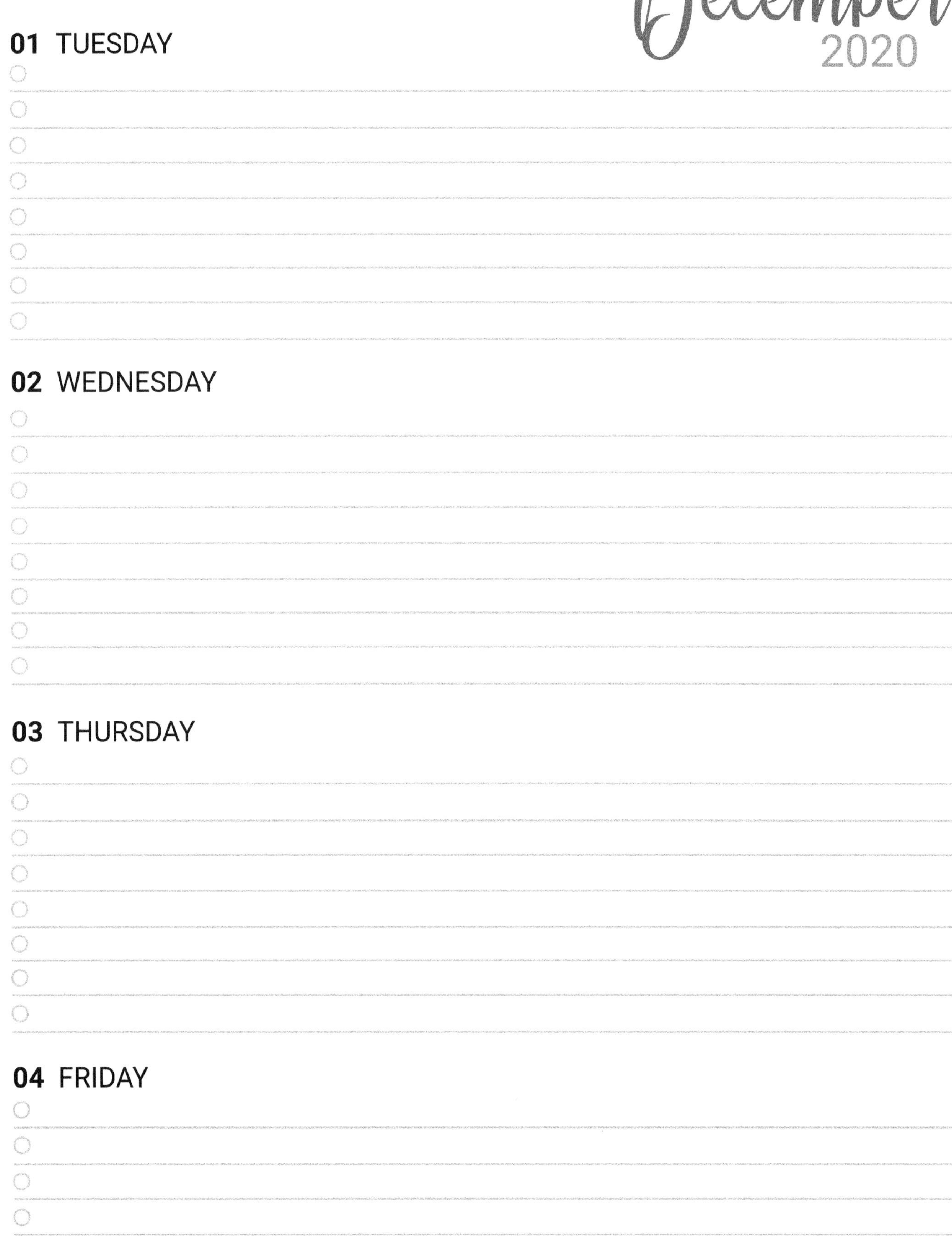

December
2020

01 TUESDAY

02 WEDNESDAY

03 THURSDAY

04 FRIDAY

December
2020

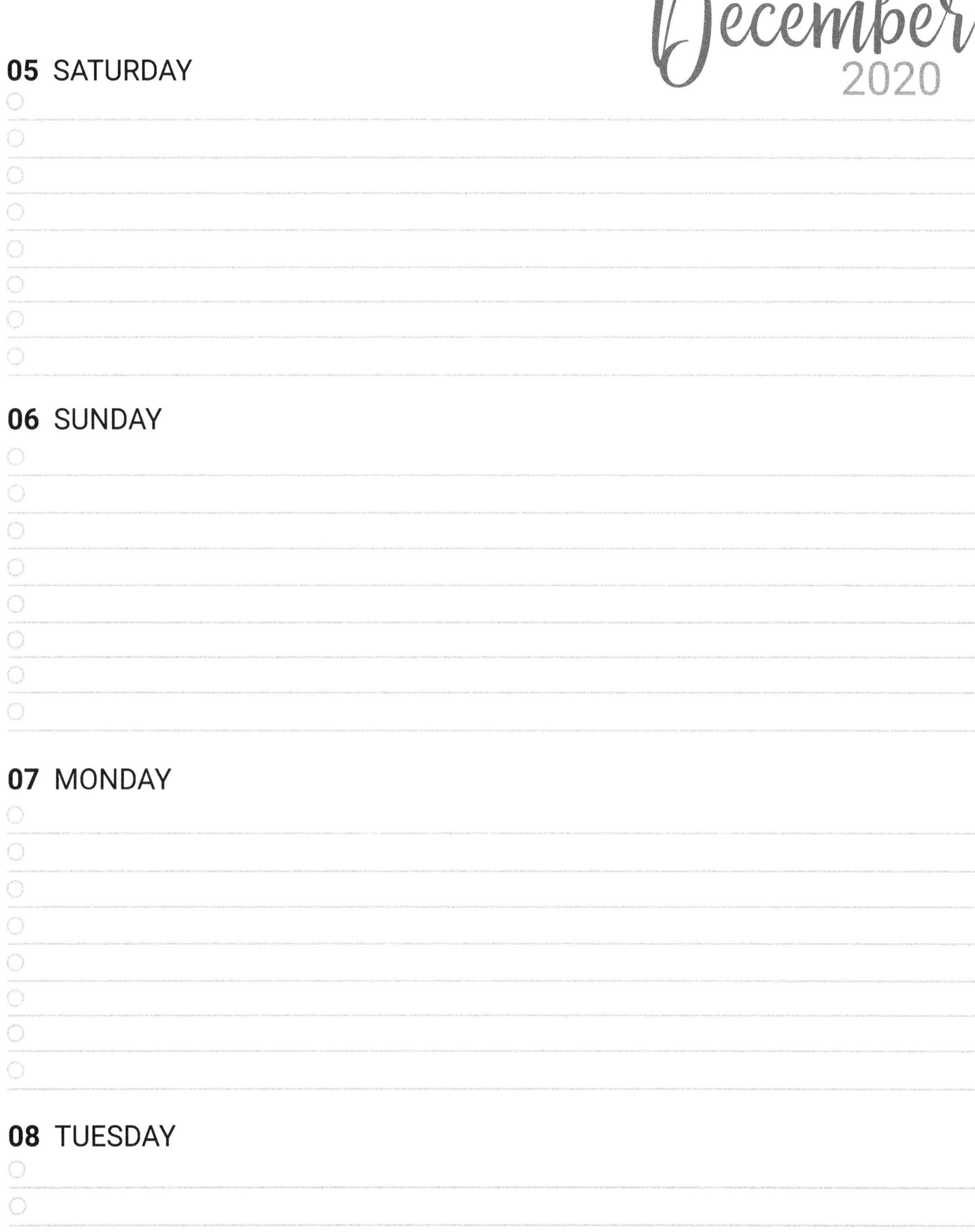

05 SATURDAY

06 SUNDAY

07 MONDAY

08 TUESDAY

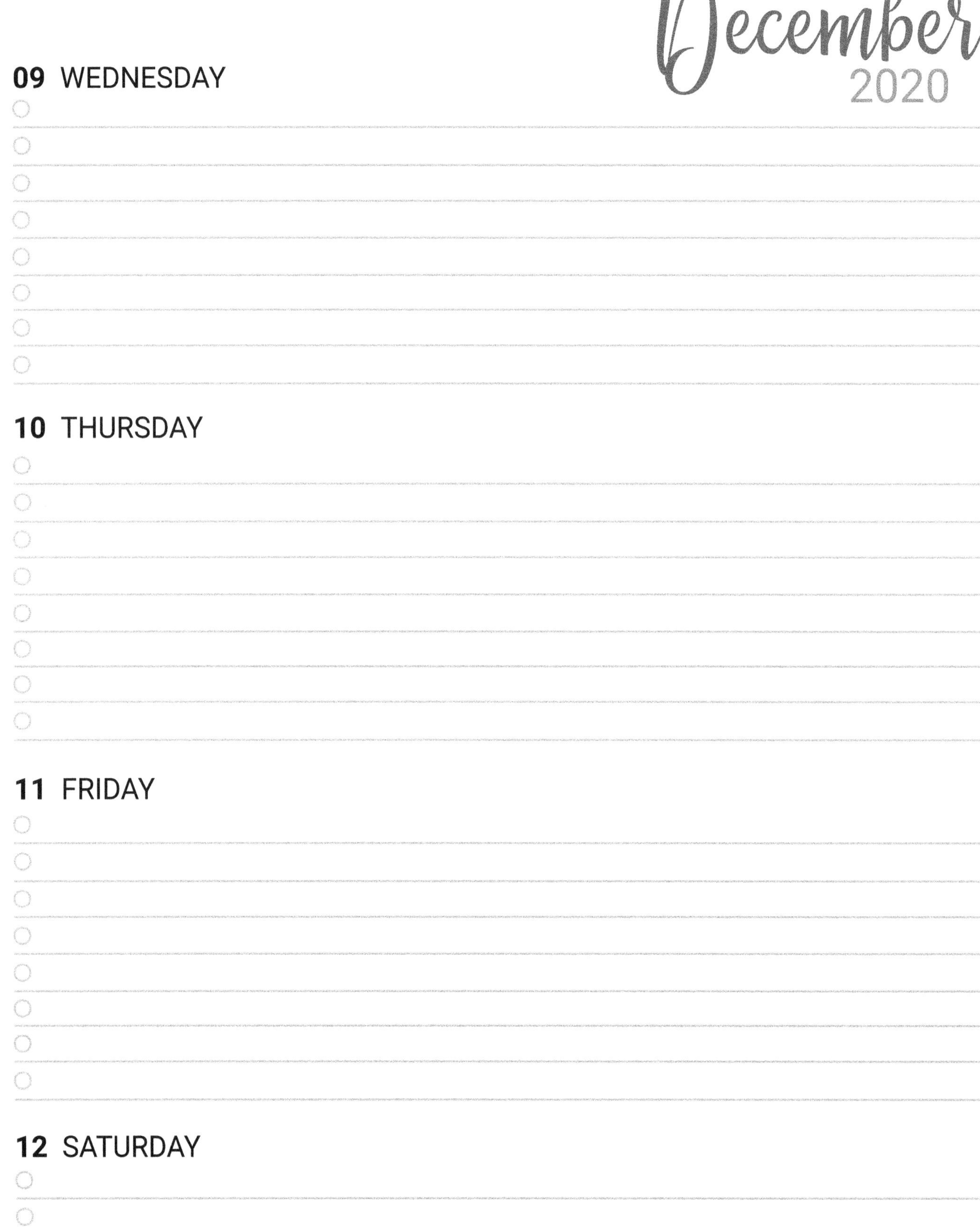

December
2020

09 WEDNESDAY

10 THURSDAY

11 FRIDAY

12 SATURDAY

December
2020

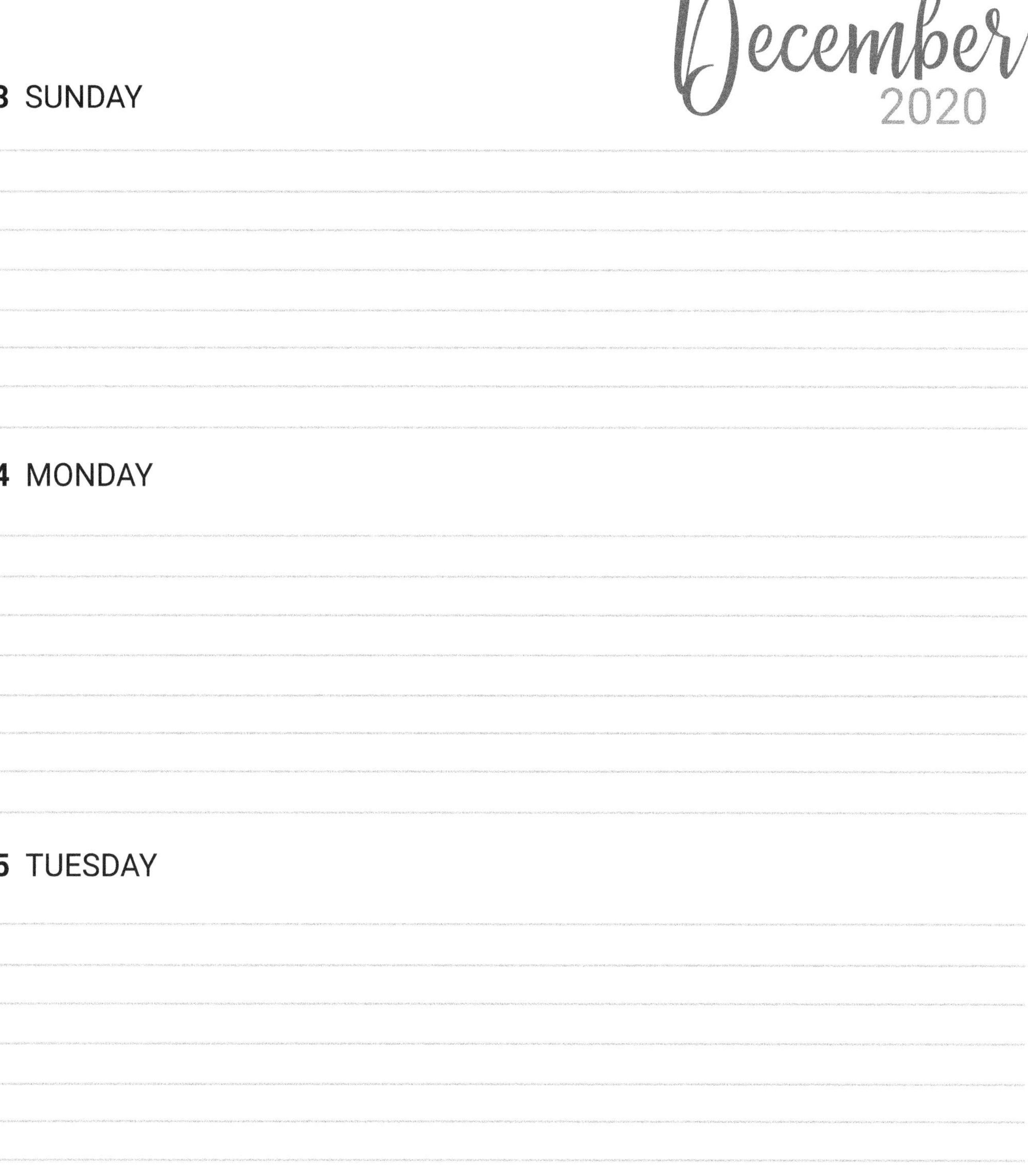

13 SUNDAY

14 MONDAY

15 TUESDAY

16 WEDNESDAY

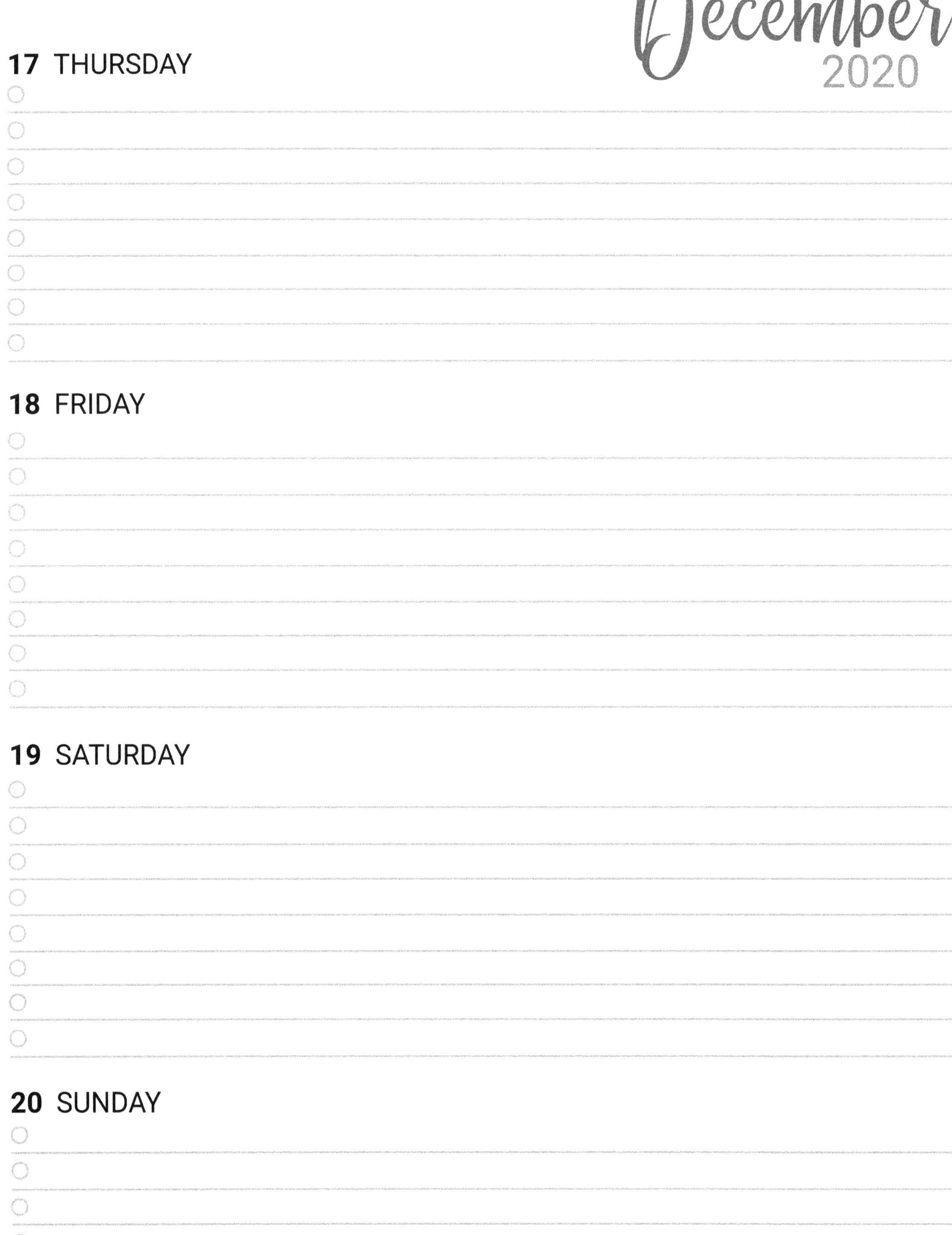

December
2020

17 THURSDAY

18 FRIDAY

19 SATURDAY

20 SUNDAY

December
2020

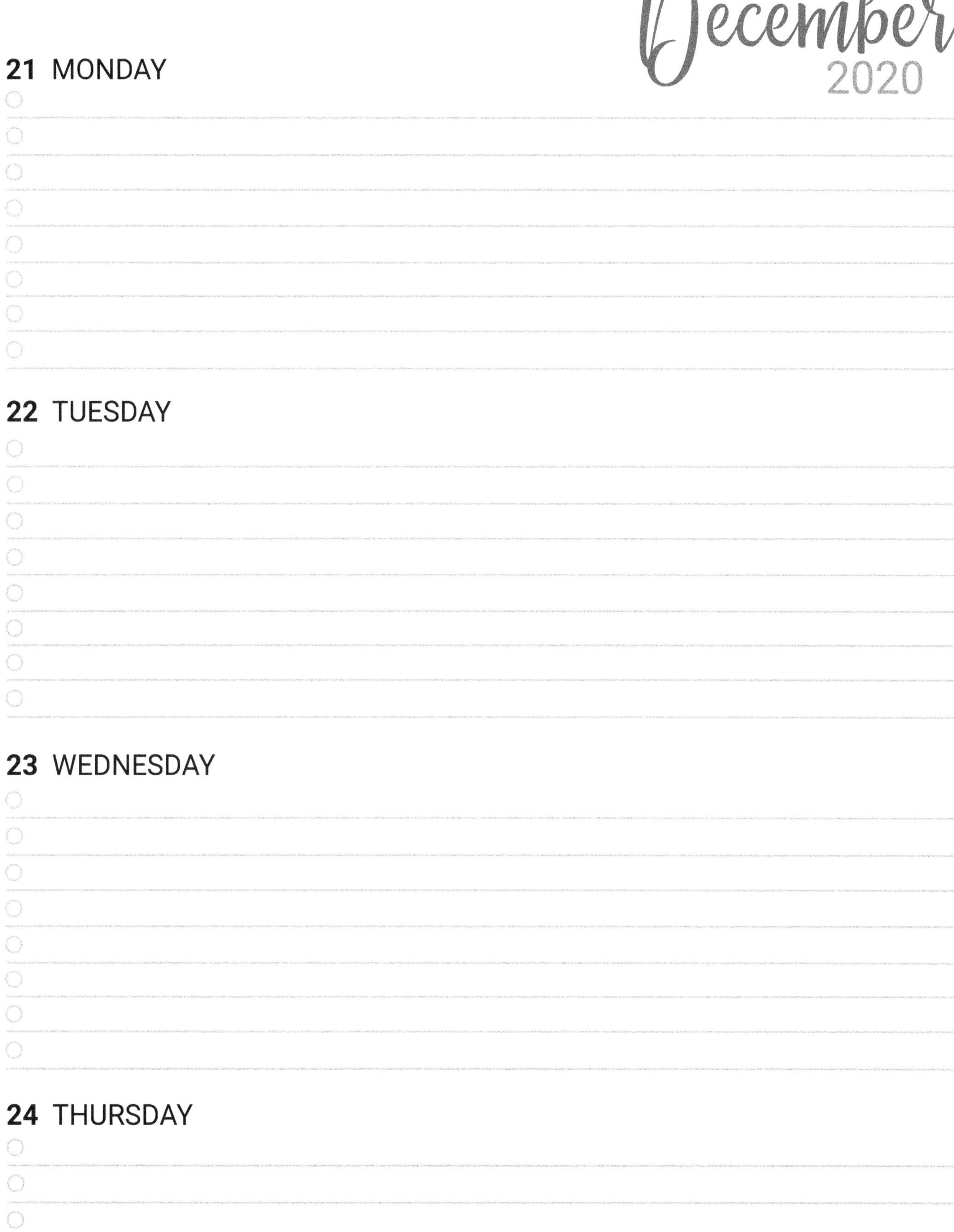

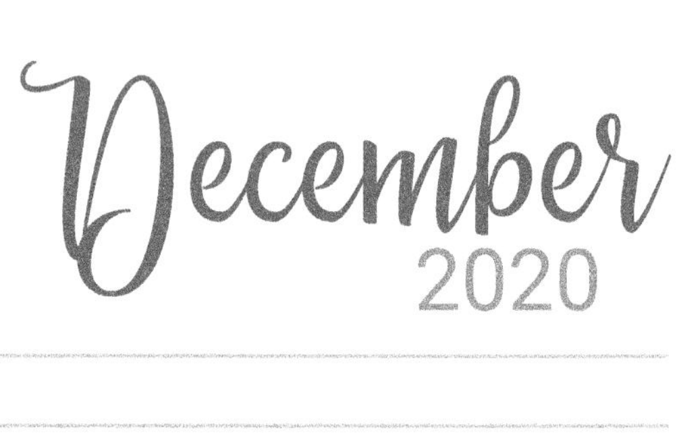

25 FRIDAY

26 SATURDAY

27 SUNDAY

28 MONDAY

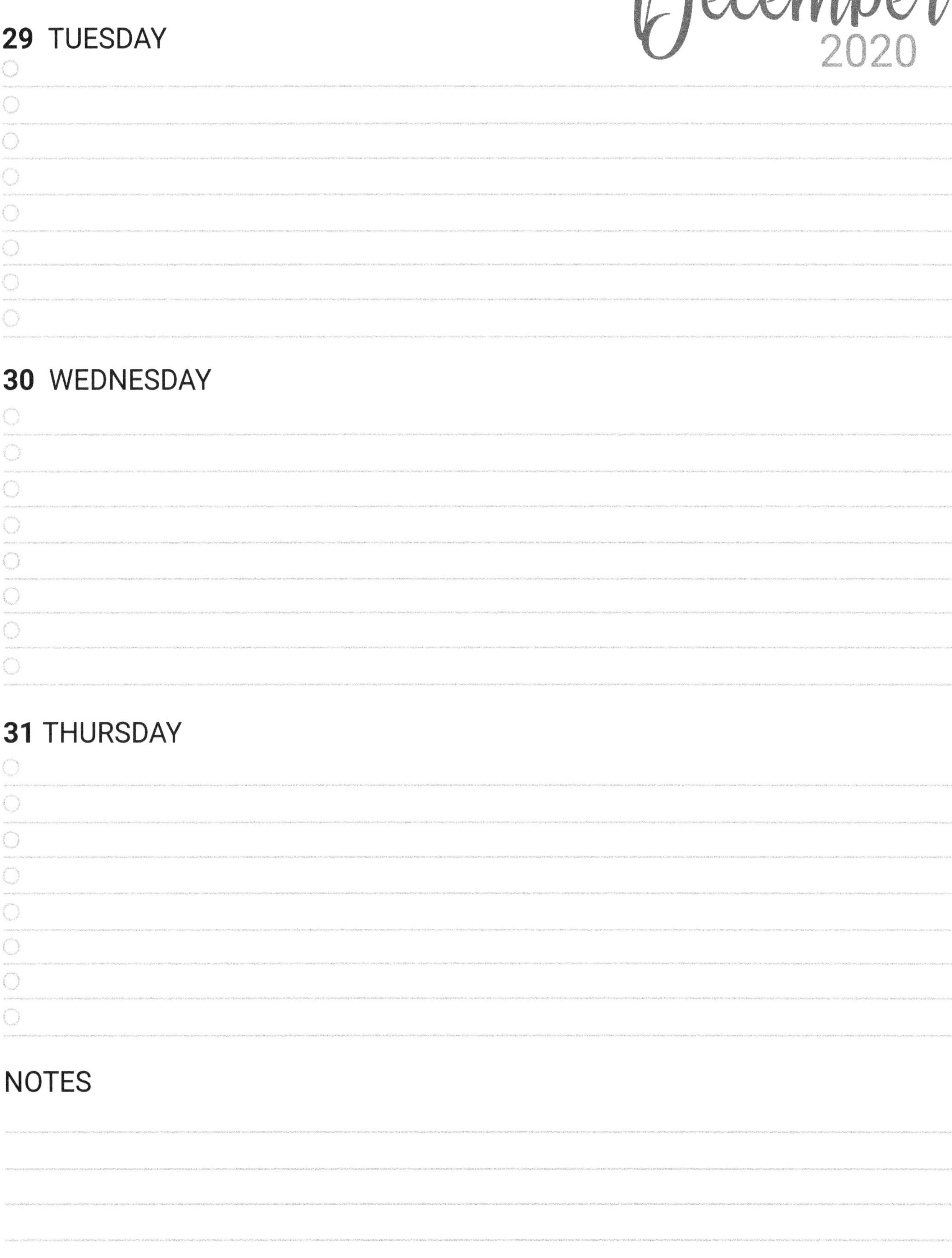

29 TUESDAY

30 WEDNESDAY

31 THURSDAY

NOTES

January
2021

01 FRIDAY

02 SATURDAY

03 SUNDAY

04 MONDAY

January
2021

05 TUESDAY

06 WEDNESDAY

07 THURSDAY

08 FRIDAY

January
2021

09 SATURDAY

○
○
○
○
○
○
○
○

10 SUNDAY

○
○
○
○
○
○
○
○

11 MONDAY

○
○
○
○
○
○
○
○

12 TUESDAY

○
○
○
○
○

January
2021

13 WEDNESDAY

14 THURSDAY

15 FRIDAY

16 SATURDAY

January
2021

17 SUNDAY

18 MONDAY

19 TUESDAY

20 WEDNESDAY

January
2021

21 THURSDAY

22 FRIDAY

23 SATURDAY

24 SUNDAY

January
2021

25 MONDAY

26 TUESDAY

27 WEDNESDAY

28 THURSDAY

January
2021

29 FRIDAY

30 SATURDAY

31 SUNDAY

NOTES

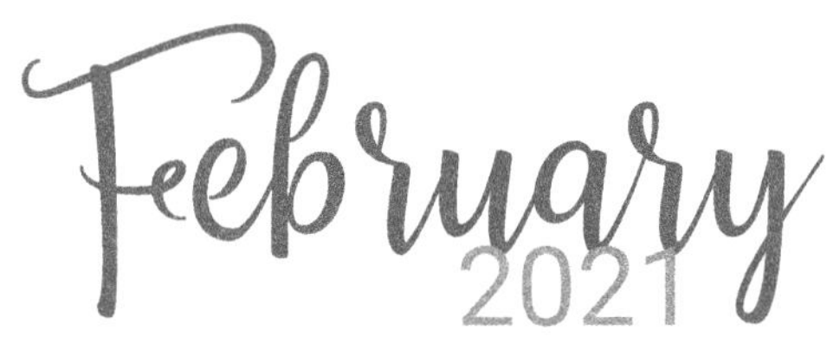

01 MONDAY

02 TUESDAY

03 WEDNESDAY

04 THURSDAY

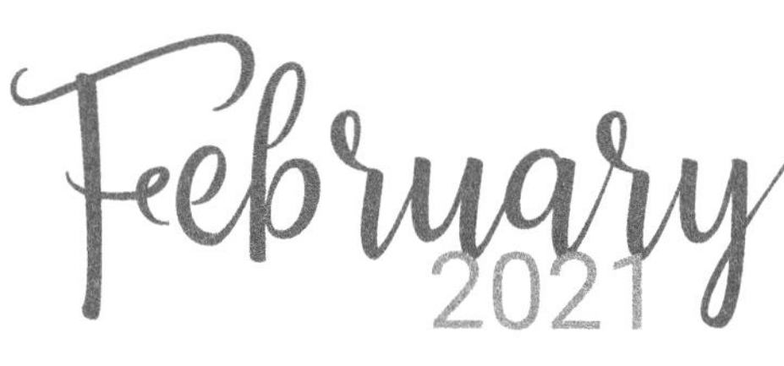

05 FRIDAY

06 SATURDAY

07 SUNDAY

08 MONDAY

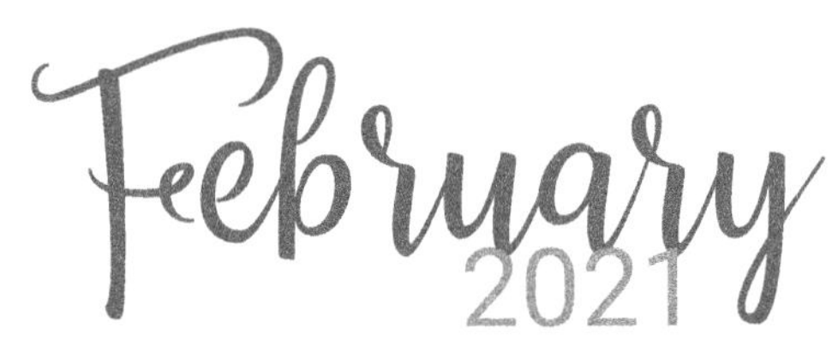

09 TUESDAY

10 WEDNESDAY

11 THURSDAY

12 FRIDAY

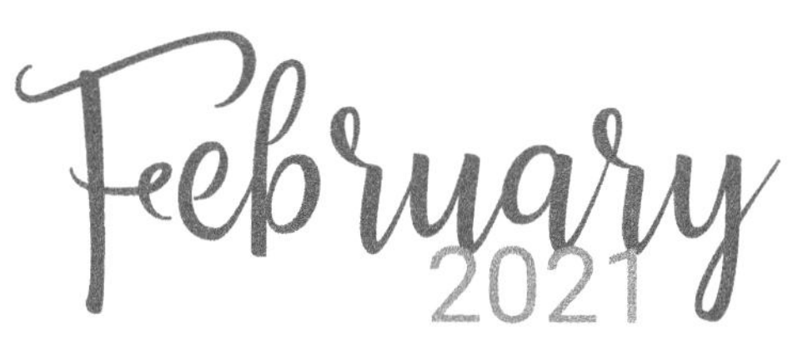

13 SATURDAY

14 SUNDAY

15 MONDAY

16 TUESDAY

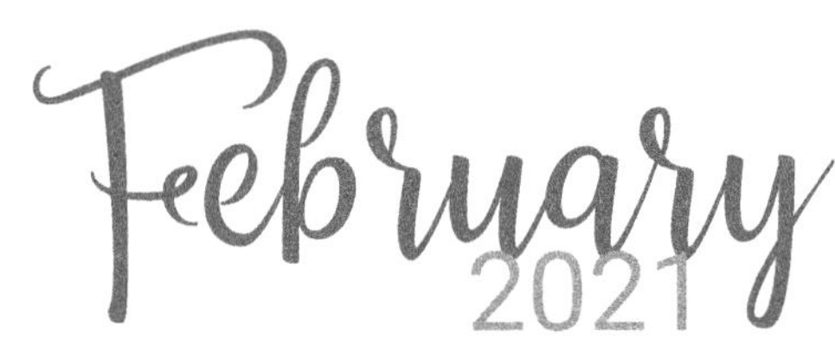

17 WEDNESDAY

18 THURSDAY

19 FRIDAY

20 SATURDAY

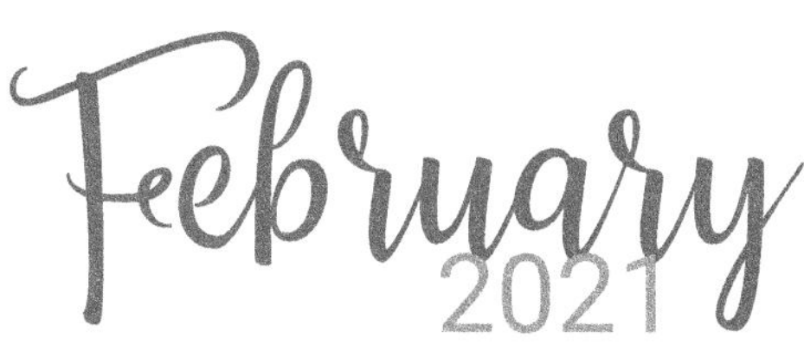

21 SUNDAY

22 MONDAY

23 TUESDAY

24 WEDNESDAY

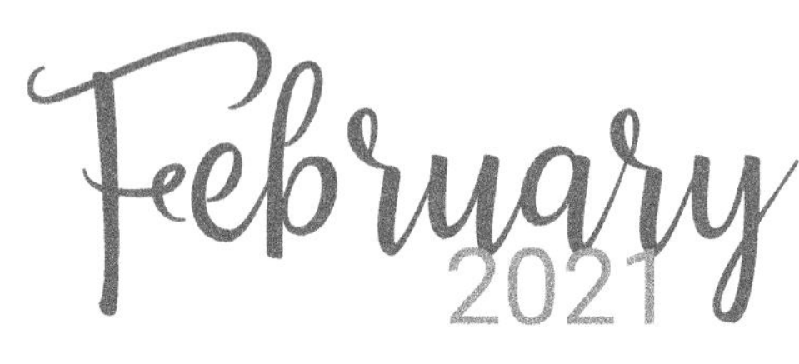

25 THURSDAY

26 FRIDAY

27 SATURDAY

28 SUNDAY

March 2021

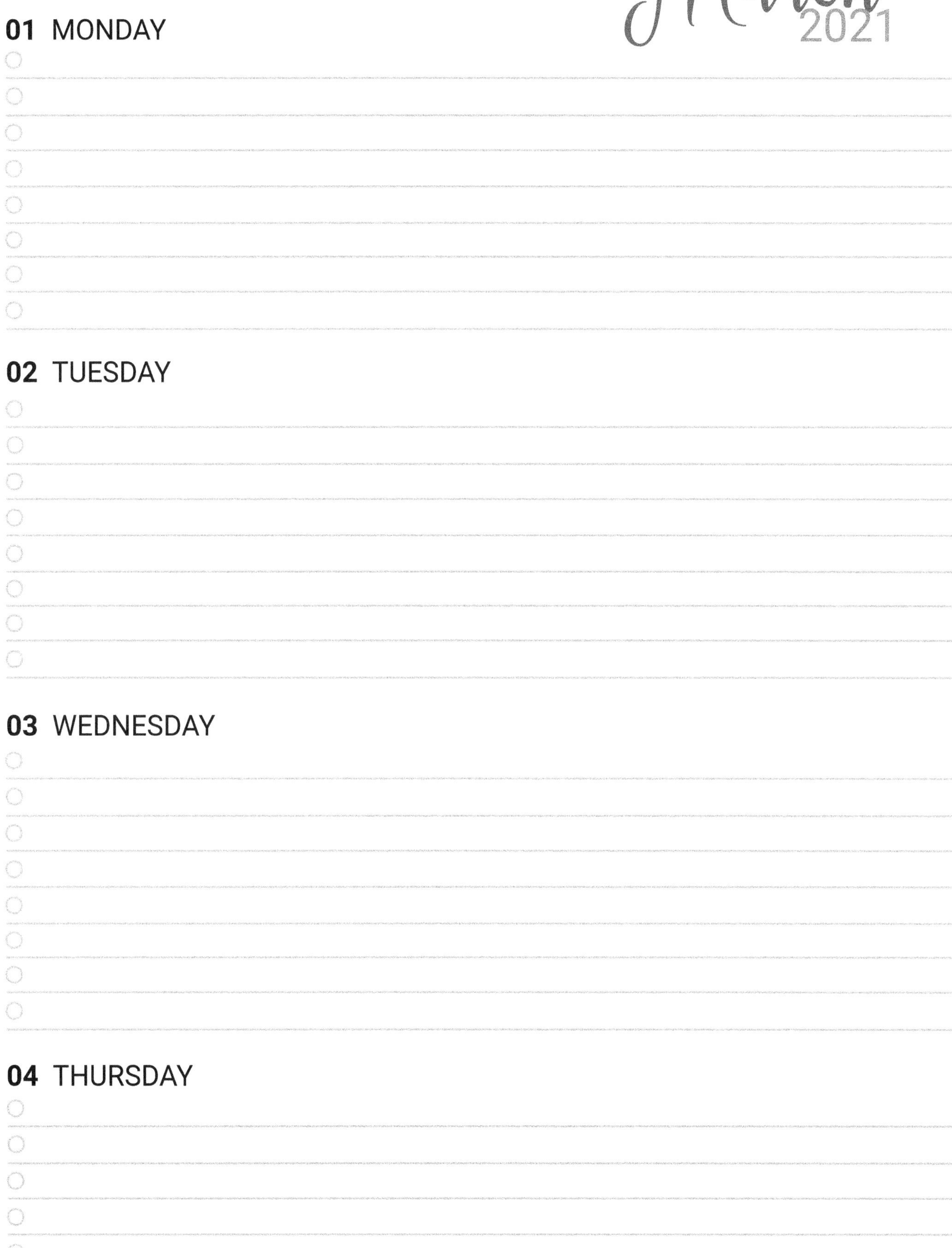

01 MONDAY

02 TUESDAY

03 WEDNESDAY

04 THURSDAY

March
2021

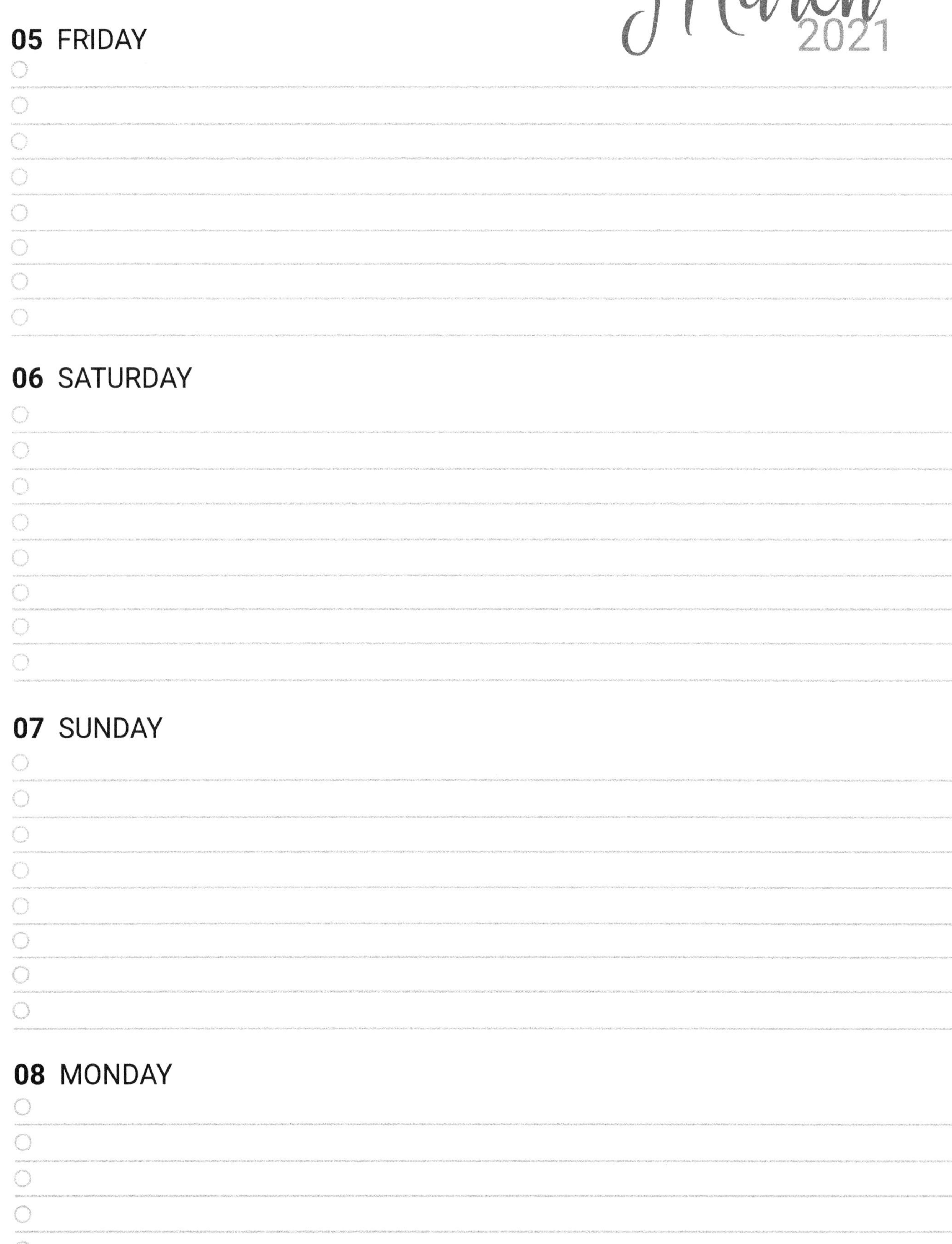

March
2021

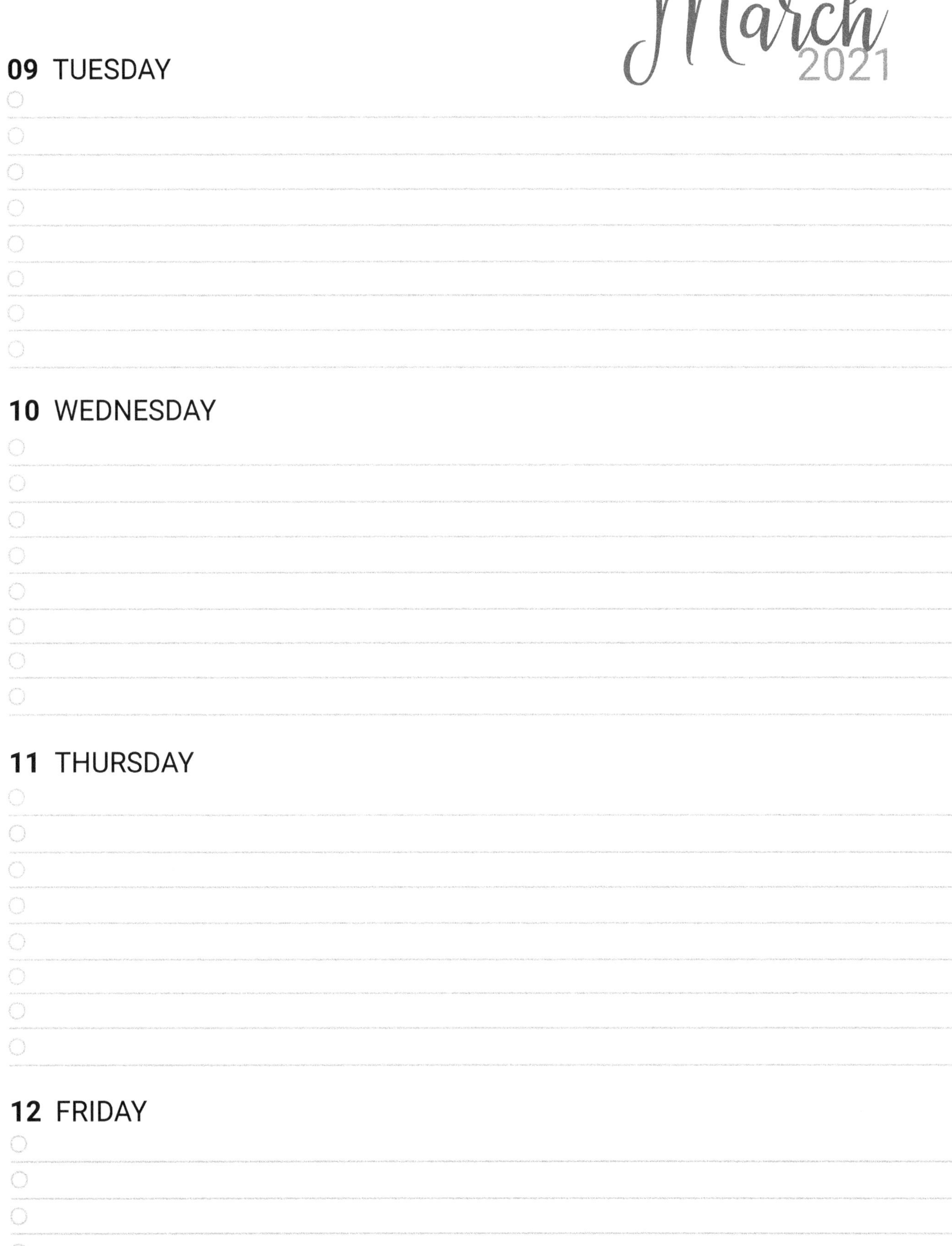

09 TUESDAY

10 WEDNESDAY

11 THURSDAY

12 FRIDAY

March
2021

13 SATURDAY

14 SUNDAY

15 MONDAY

16 TUESDAY

March 2021

17 WEDNESDAY

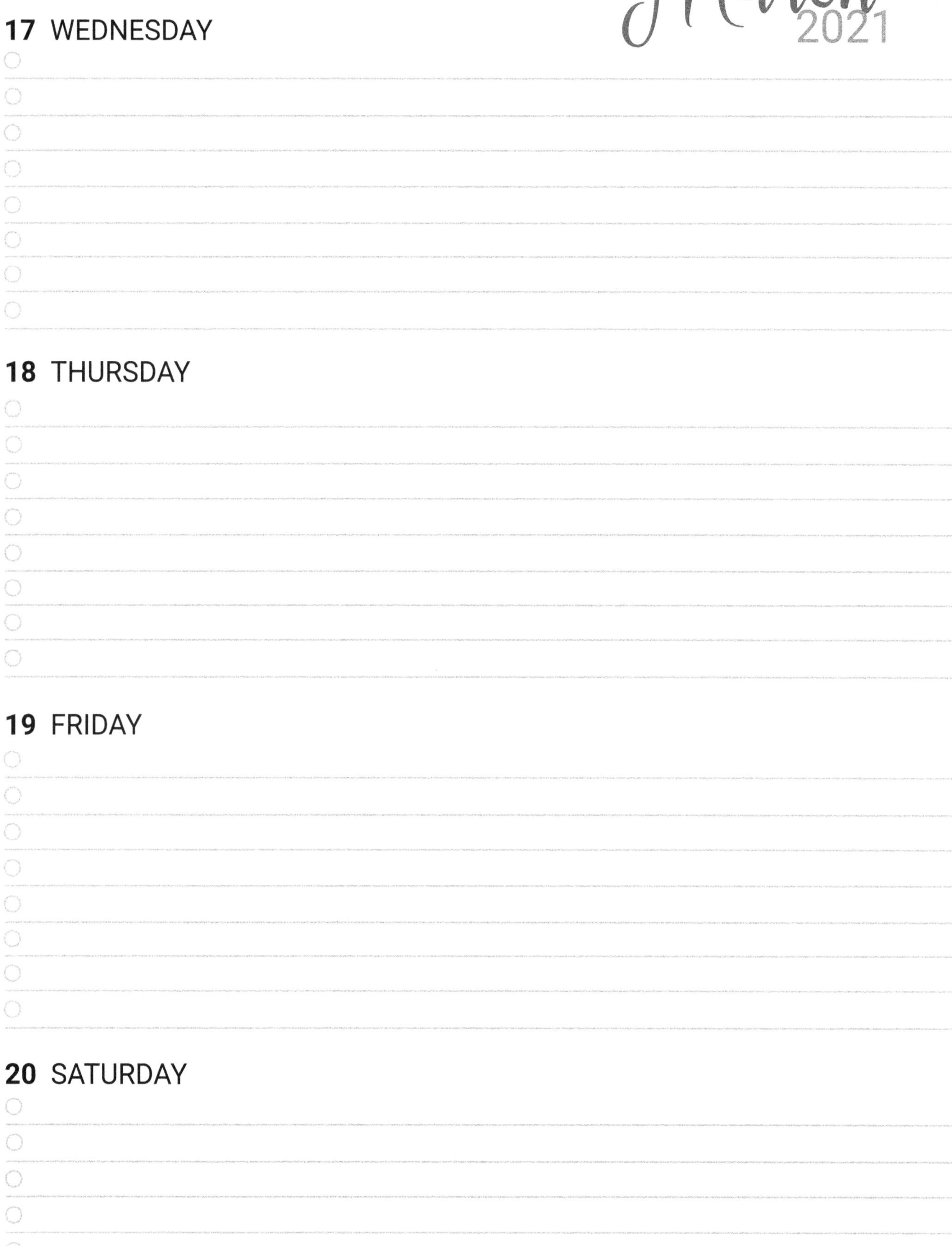

18 THURSDAY

19 FRIDAY

20 SATURDAY

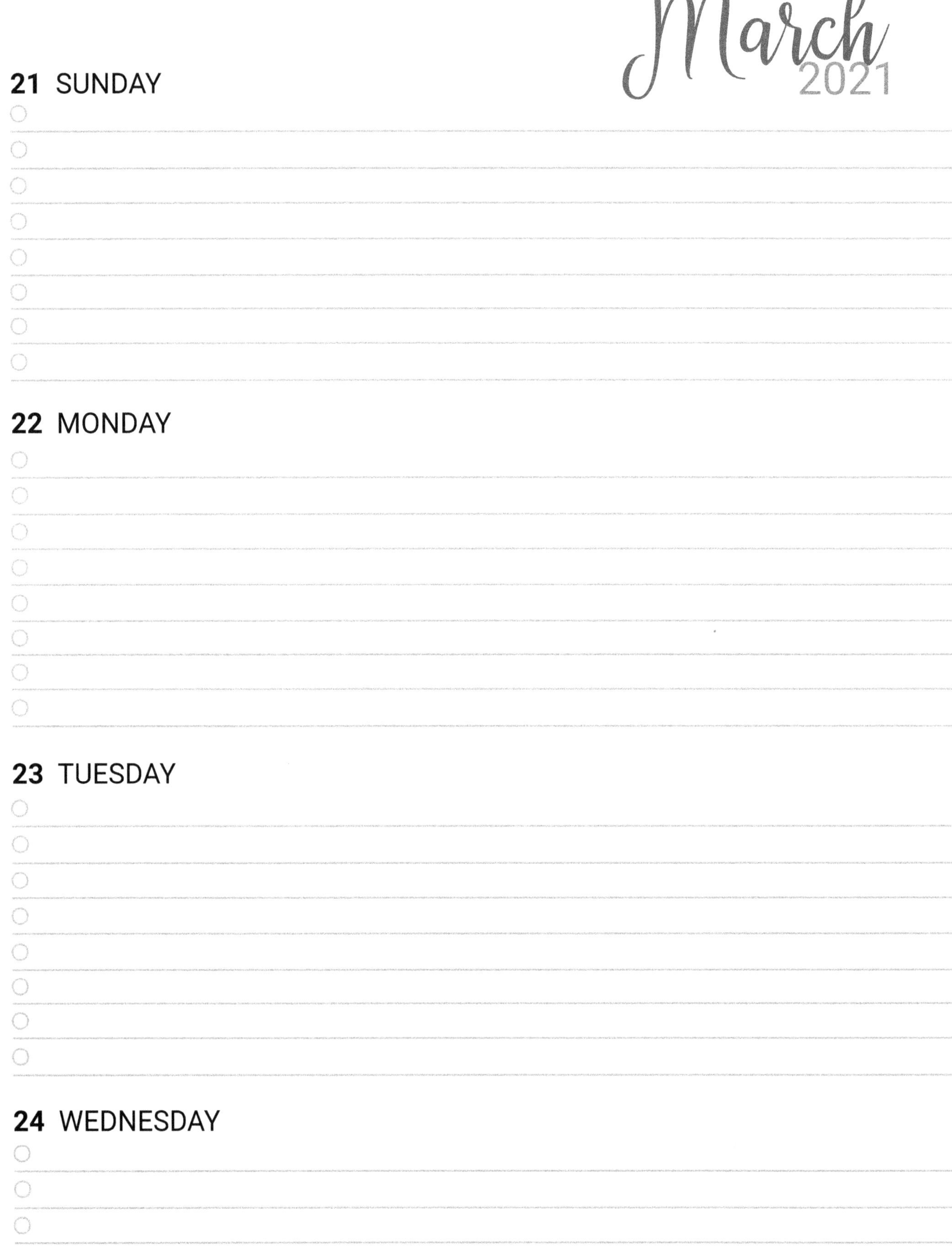

March 2021

21 SUNDAY

22 MONDAY

23 TUESDAY

24 WEDNESDAY

March
2021

25 THURSDAY

26 FRIDAY

27 SATURDAY

28 SUNDAY

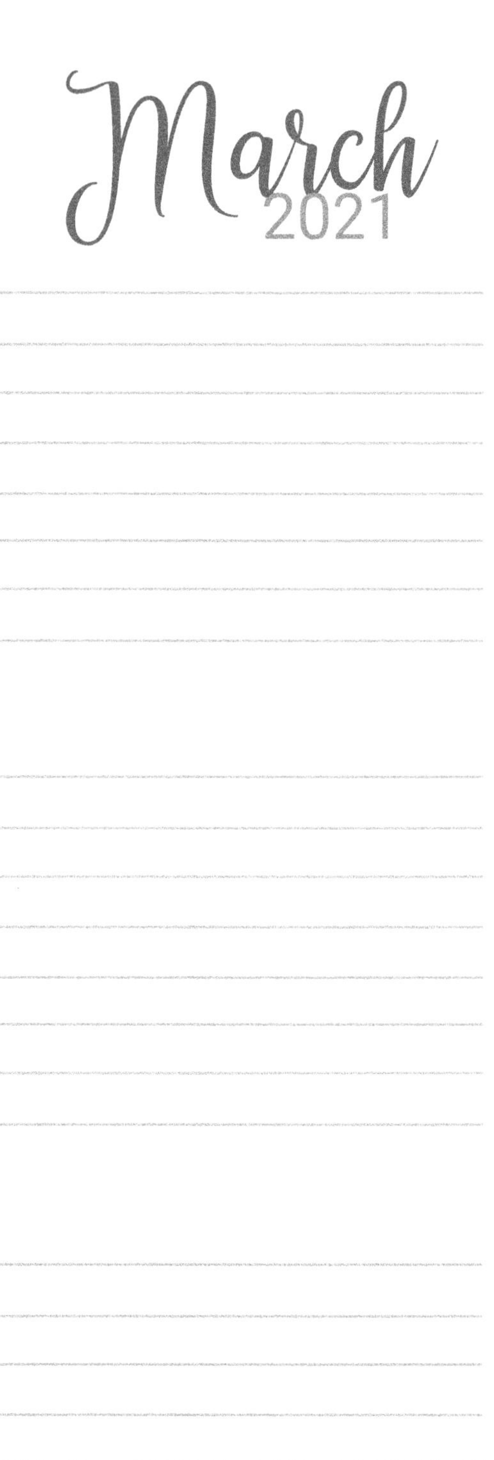

29 MONDAY

30 TUESDAY

31 WEDNESDAY

NOTES

April 2021

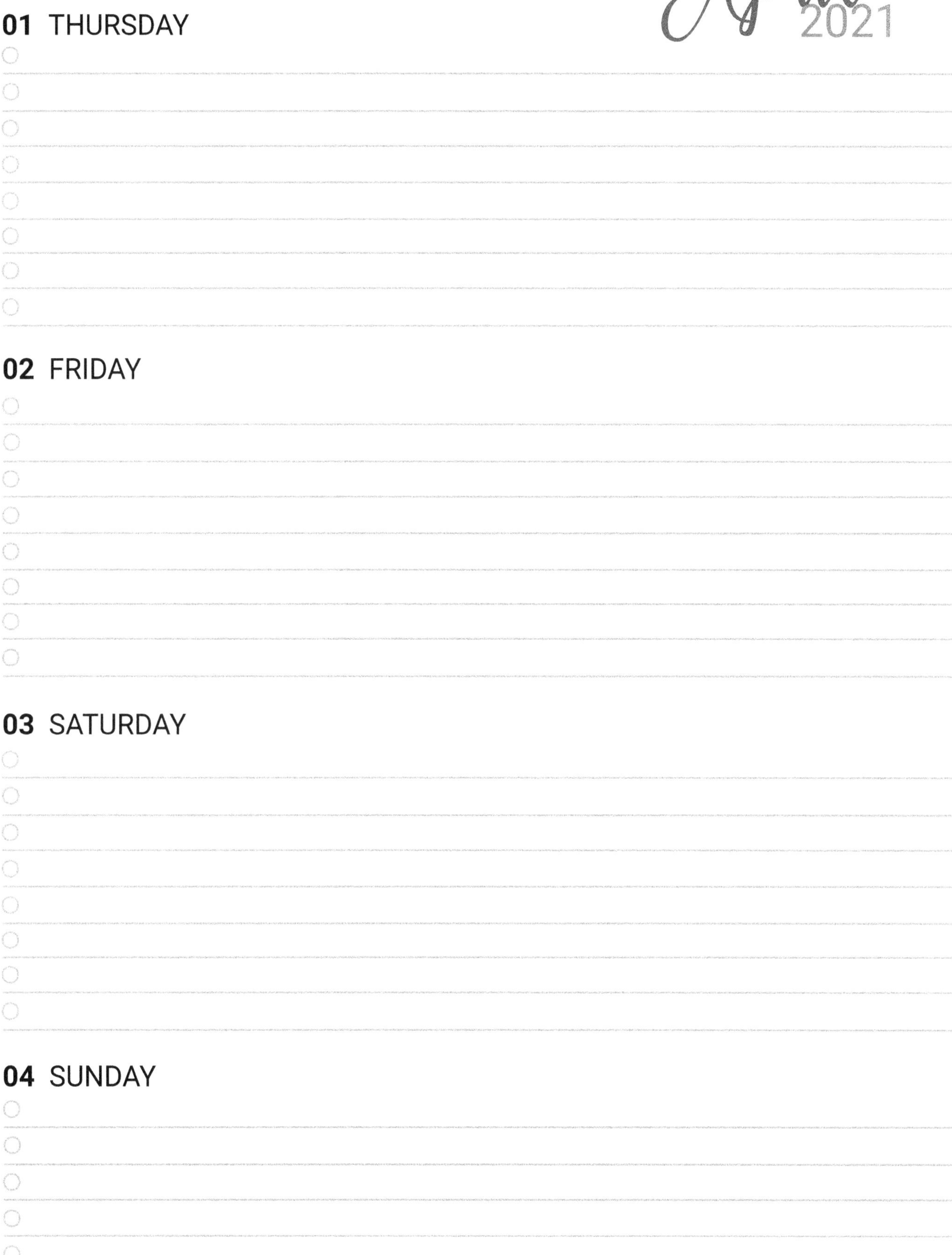

01 THURSDAY

02 FRIDAY

03 SATURDAY

04 SUNDAY

April 2021

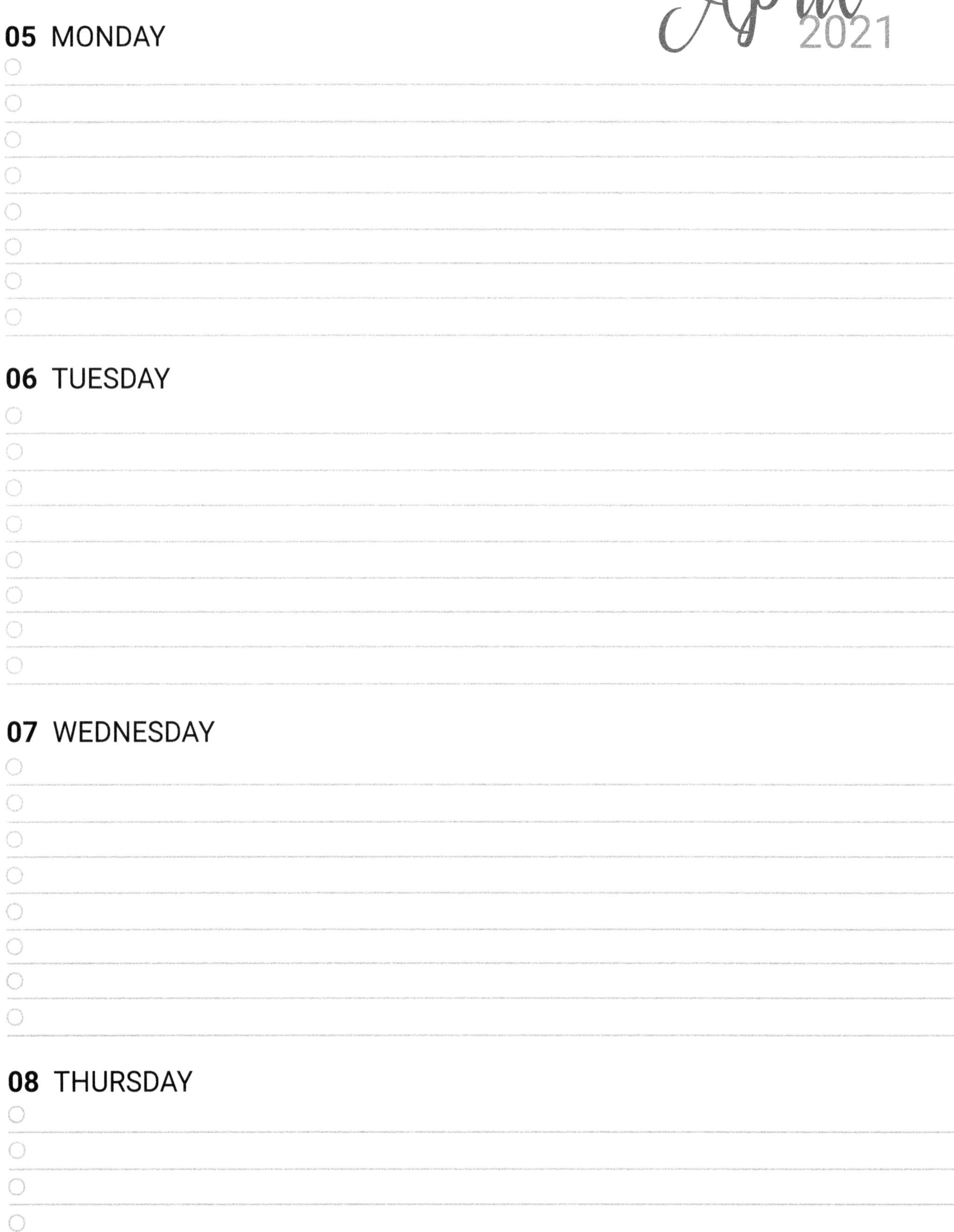

05 MONDAY

06 TUESDAY

07 WEDNESDAY

08 THURSDAY

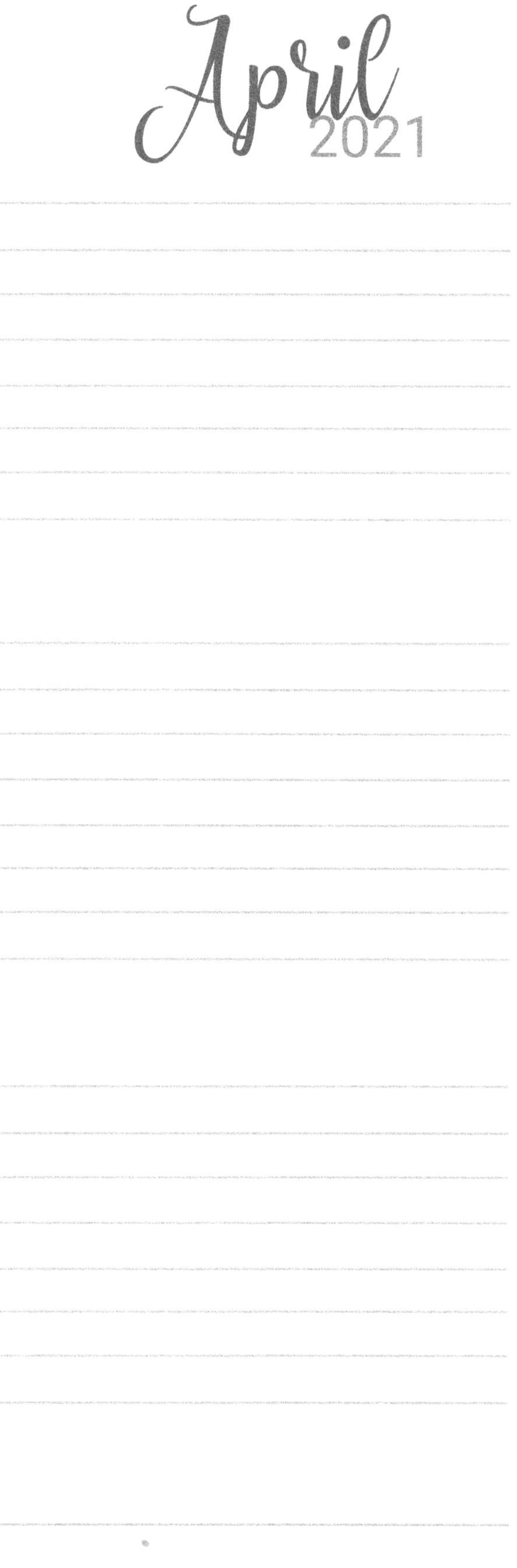

09 FRIDAY

10 SATURDAY

11 SUNDAY

12 MONDAY

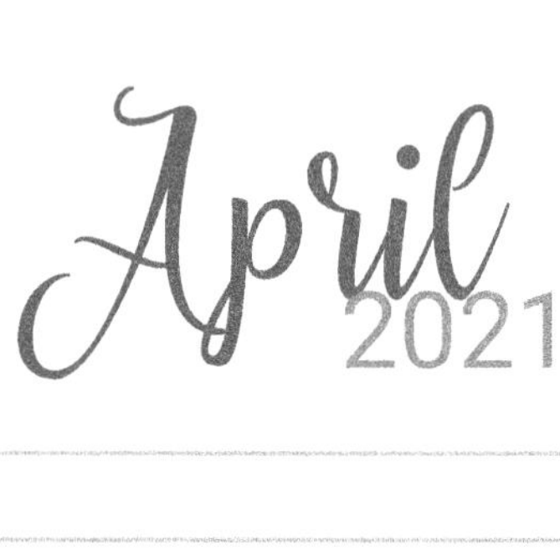

13 TUESDAY

14 WEDNESDAY

15 THURSDAY

16 FRIDAY

17 SATURDAY

18 SUNDAY

19 MONDAY

20 TUESDAY

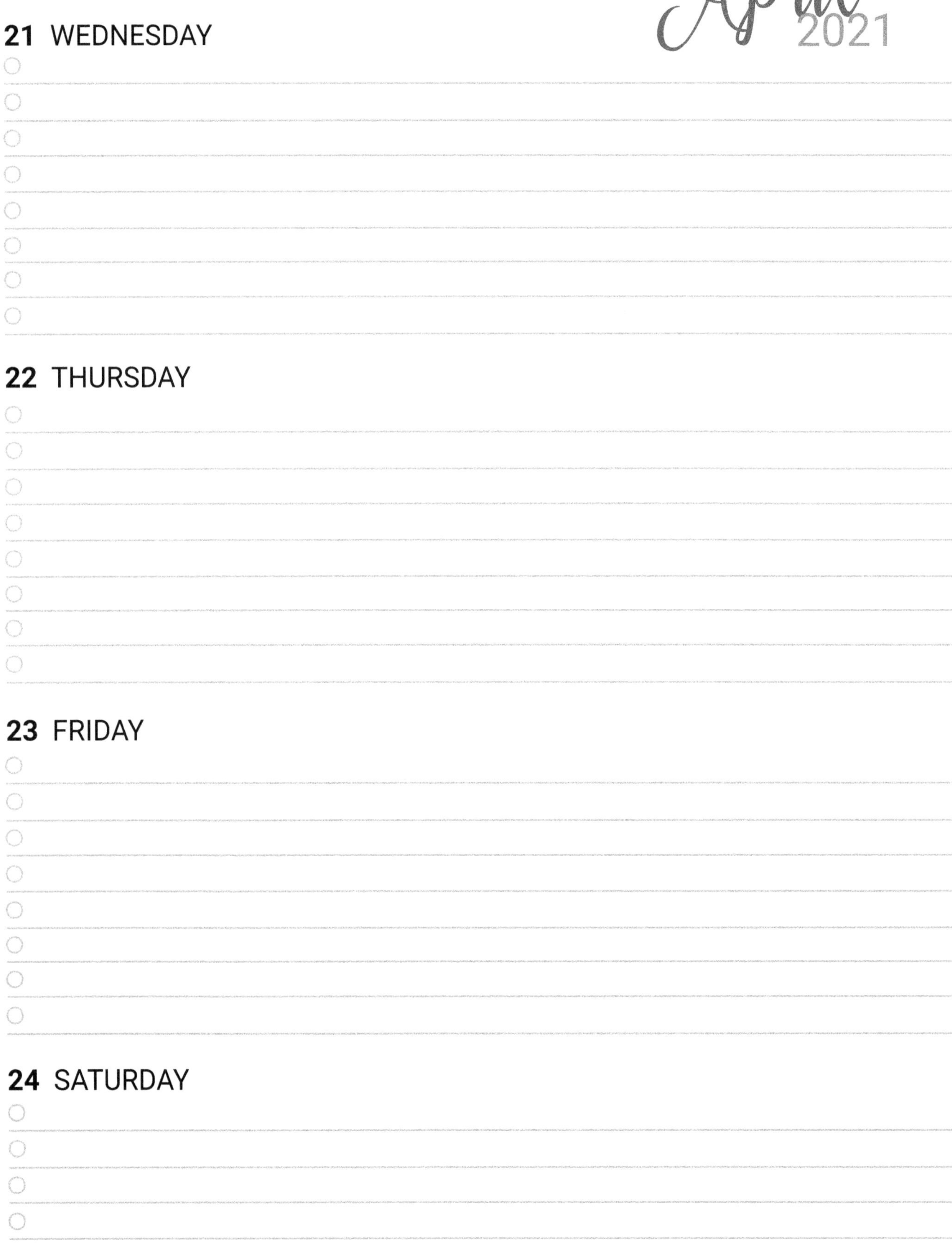

April 2021

21 WEDNESDAY

22 THURSDAY

23 FRIDAY

24 SATURDAY

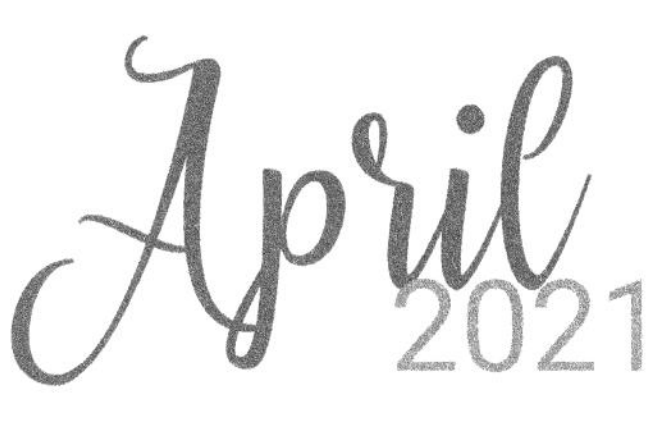

25 SUNDAY

26 MONDAY

27 TUESDAY

28 WEDNESDAY

April
2021

29 THURSDAY

30 FRIDAY

NOTES

May
2021

01 SATURDAY

02 SUNDAY

03 MONDAY

04 TUESDAY

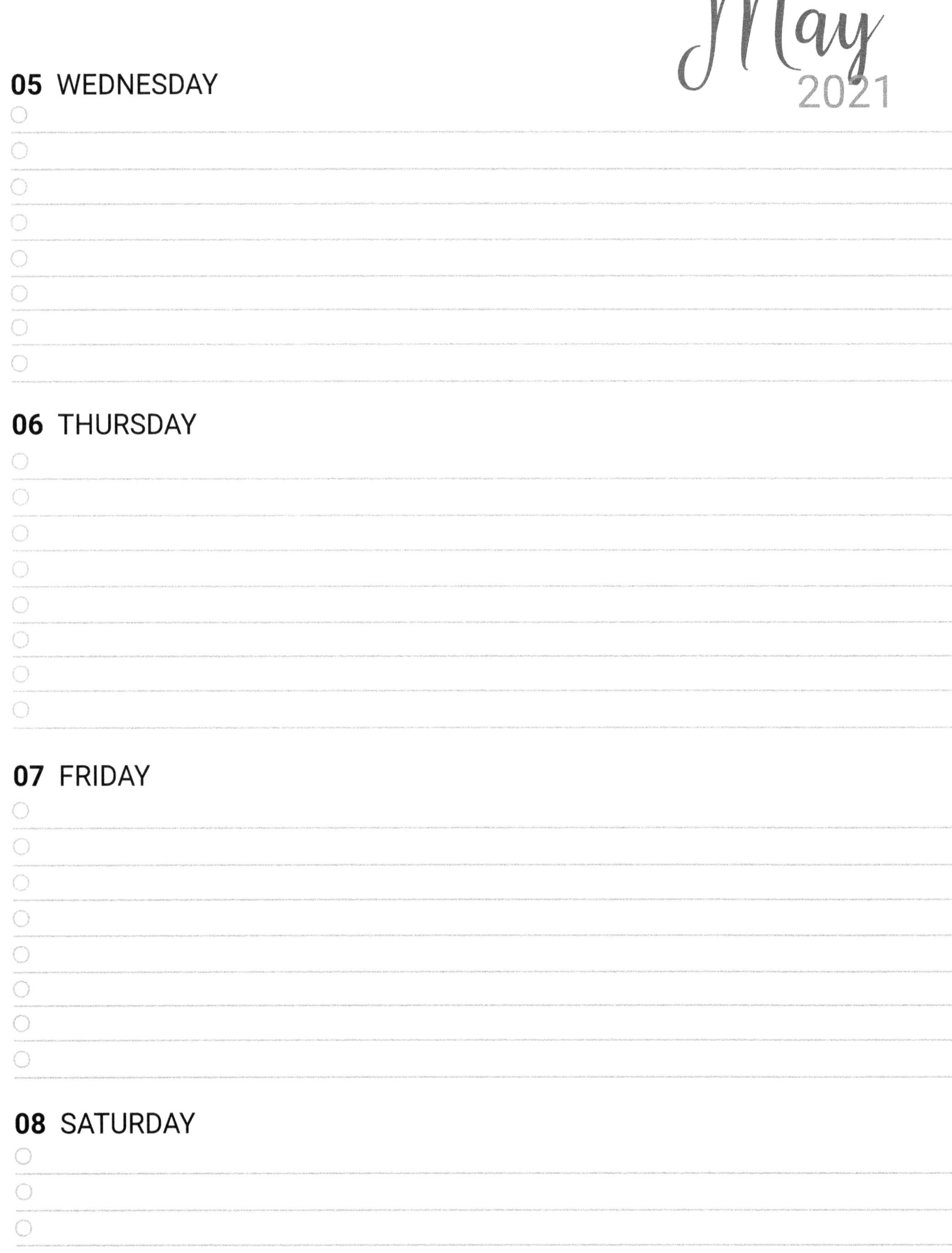

May
2021

05 WEDNESDAY

06 THURSDAY

07 FRIDAY

08 SATURDAY

09 SUNDAY

10 MONDAY

11 TUESDAY

12 WEDNESDAY

May
2021

13 THURSDAY

14 FRIDAY

15 SATURDAY

16 SUNDAY

May
2021

17 MONDAY

18 TUESDAY

19 WEDNESDAY

20 THURSDAY

May 2021

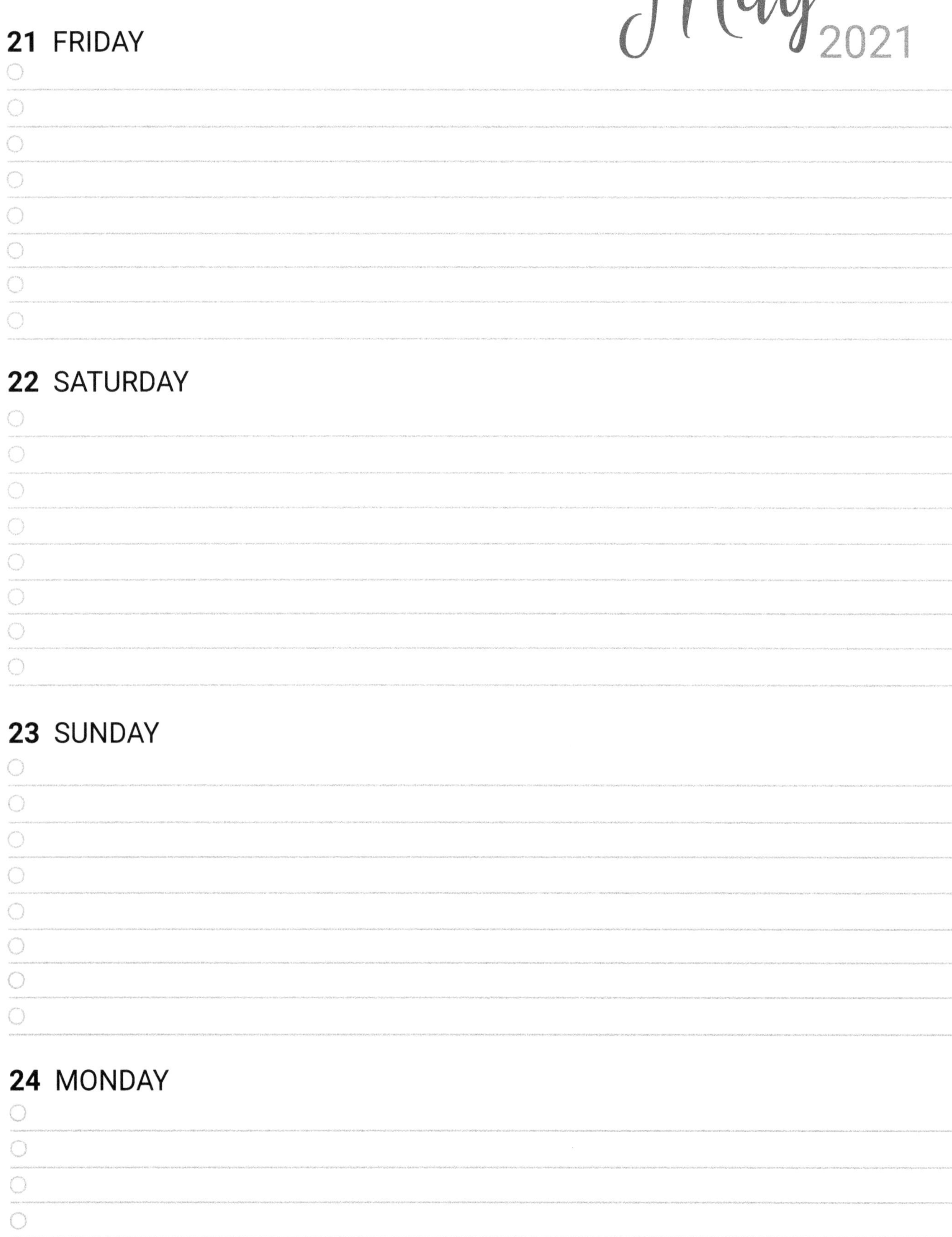

21 FRIDAY

22 SATURDAY

23 SUNDAY

24 MONDAY

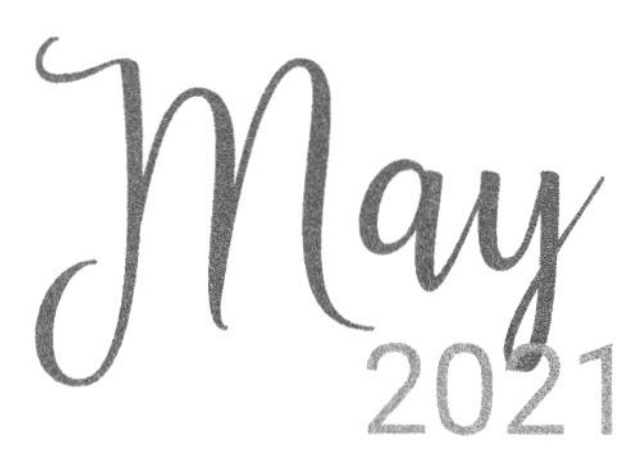

25 TUESDAY

26 WEDNESDAY

27 THURSDAY

28 FRIDAY

May 2021

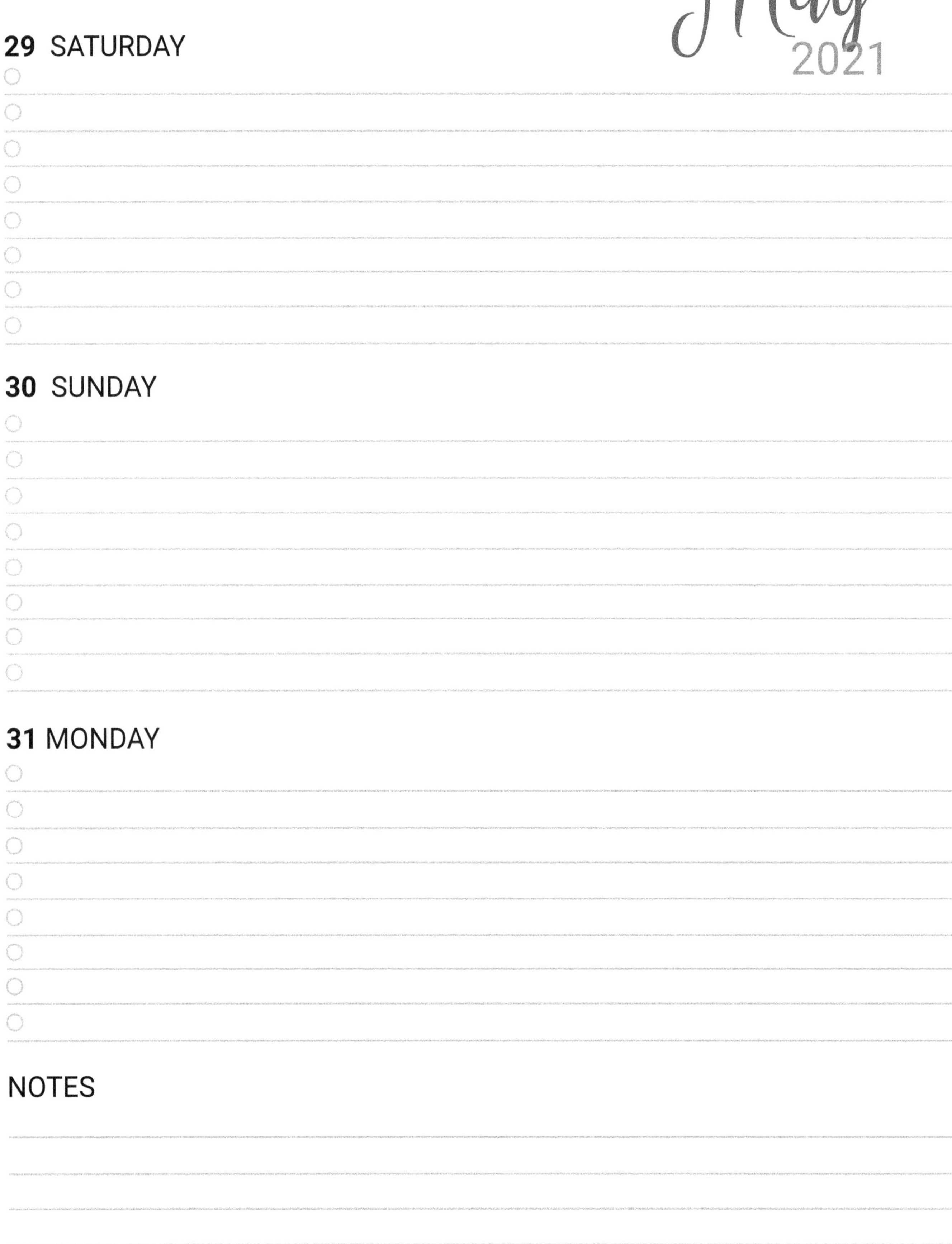

29 SATURDAY

30 SUNDAY

31 MONDAY

NOTES

June 2021

01 TUESDAY

02 WEDNESDAY

03 THURSDAY

04 FRIDAY

June 2021

05 SATURDAY

06 SUNDAY

07 MONDAY

08 TUESDAY

June 2021

09 WEDNESDAY

10 THURSDAY

11 FRIDAY

12 SATURDAY

June 2021

13 SUNDAY

14 MONDAY

15 TUESDAY

16 WEDNESDAY

June 2021

17 THURSDAY

18 FRIDAY

19 SATURDAY

20 SUNDAY

June 2021

21 MONDAY

22 TUESDAY

23 WEDNESDAY

24 THURSDAY

June 2021

25 FRIDAY

26 SATURDAY

27 SUNDAY

28 MONDAY

29 TUESDAY

30 WEDNESDAY

NOTES

July
2021

01 THURSDAY

02 FRIDAY

03 SATURDAY

04 SUNDAY

July
2021

05 MONDAY

06 TUESDAY

07 WEDNESDAY

08 THURSDAY

July
2021

09 FRIDAY

10 SATURDAY

11 SUNDAY

12 MONDAY

13 TUESDAY

14 WEDNESDAY

15 THURSDAY

16 FRIDAY

July
2021

17 SATURDAY

18 SUNDAY

19 MONDAY

20 TUESDAY

July 2021

21 WEDNESDAY

22 THURSDAY

23 FRIDAY

24 SATURDAY

July
2021

25 SUNDAY

26 MONDAY

27 TUESDAY

28 WEDNESDAY

July
2021

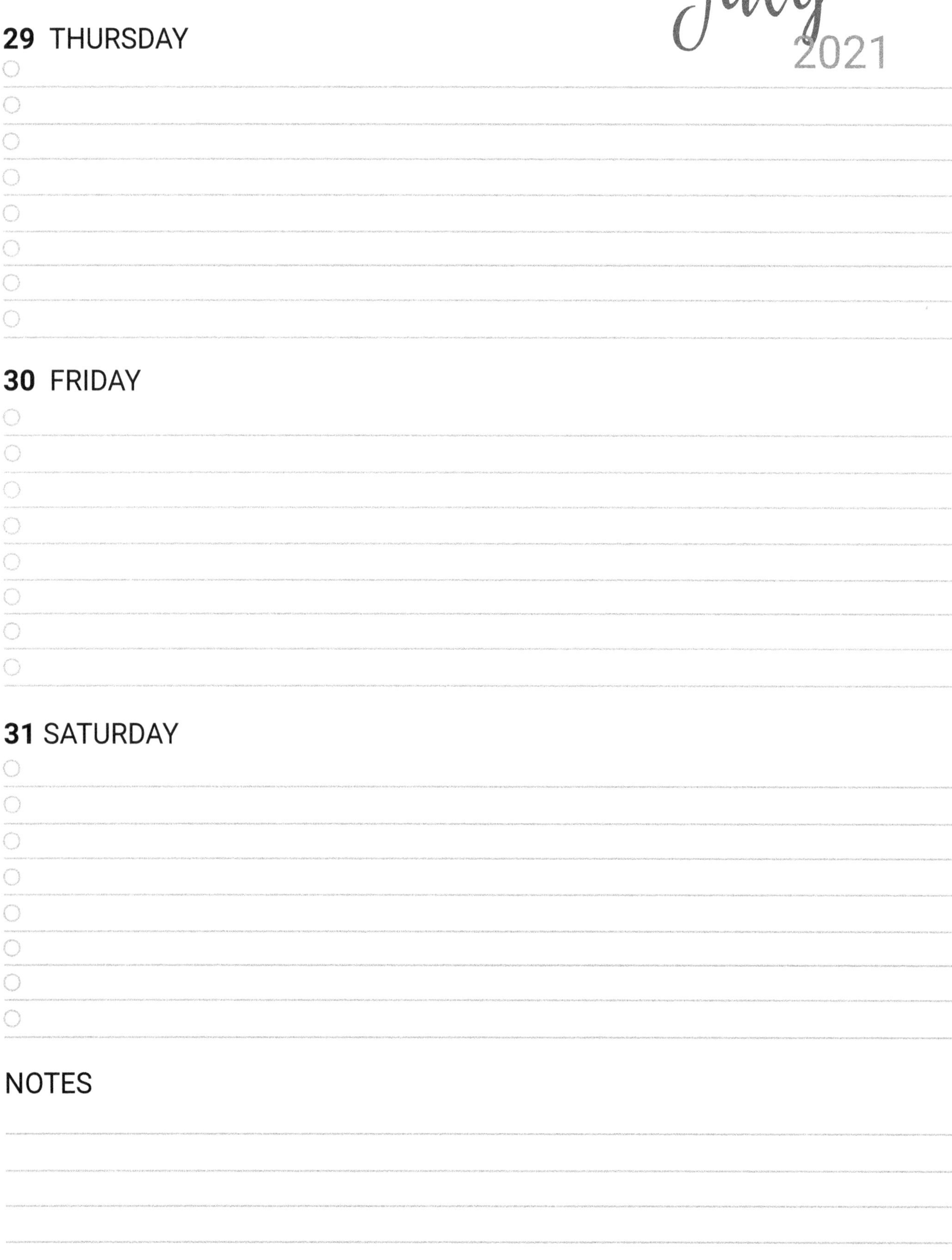

29 THURSDAY

30 FRIDAY

31 SATURDAY

NOTES

August
2021

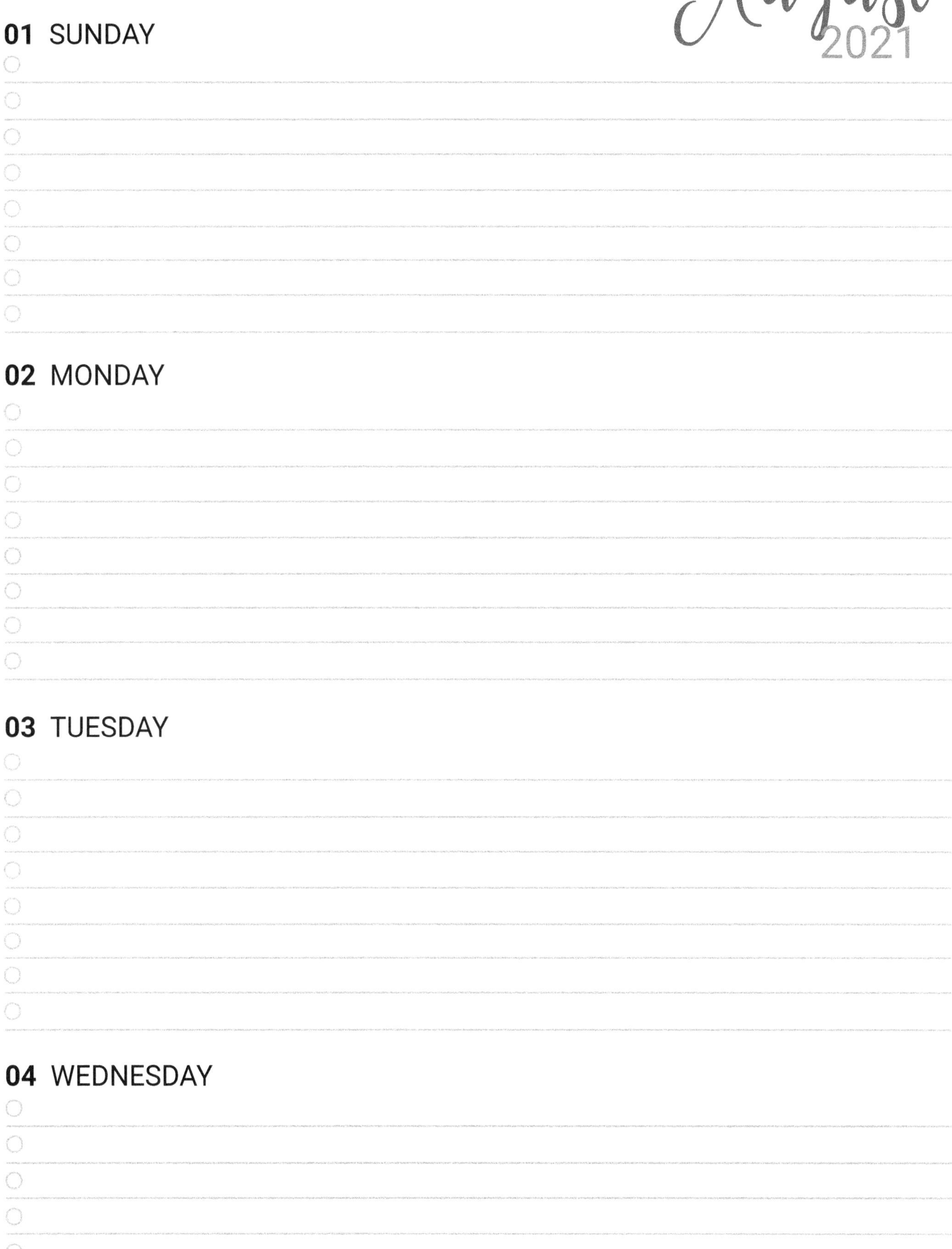

01 SUNDAY

02 MONDAY

03 TUESDAY

04 WEDNESDAY

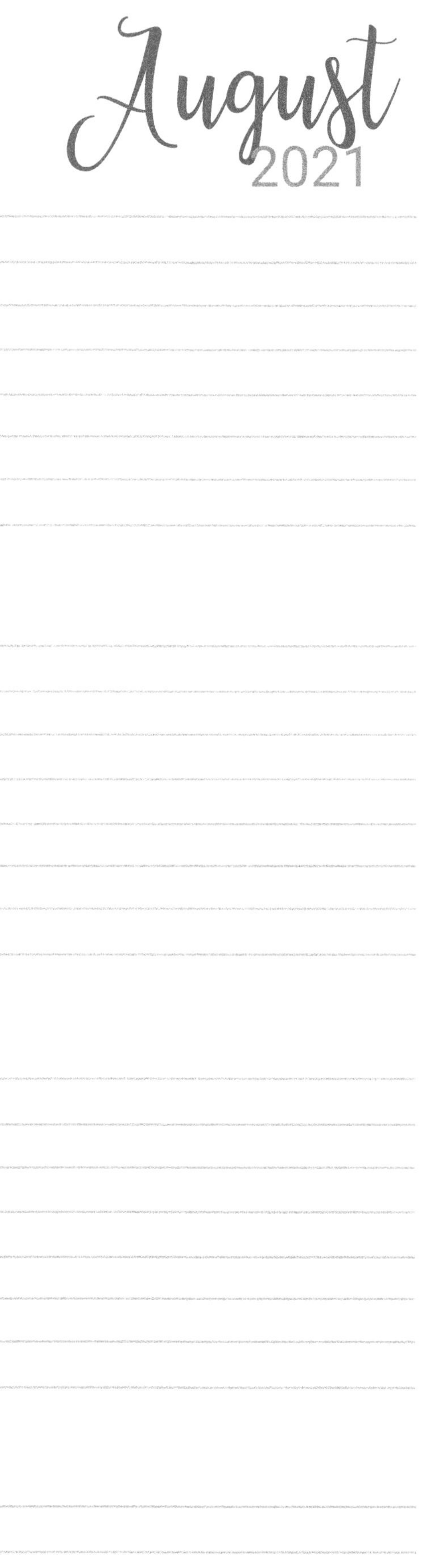

05 THURSDAY

06 FRIDAY

07 SATURDAY

08 SUNDAY

09 MONDAY

10 TUESDAY

11 WEDNESDAY

12 THURSDAY

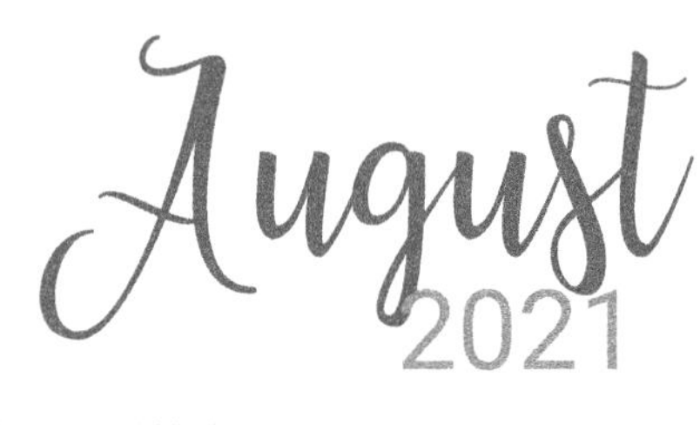

13 FRIDAY

14 SATURDAY

15 SUNDAY

16 MONDAY

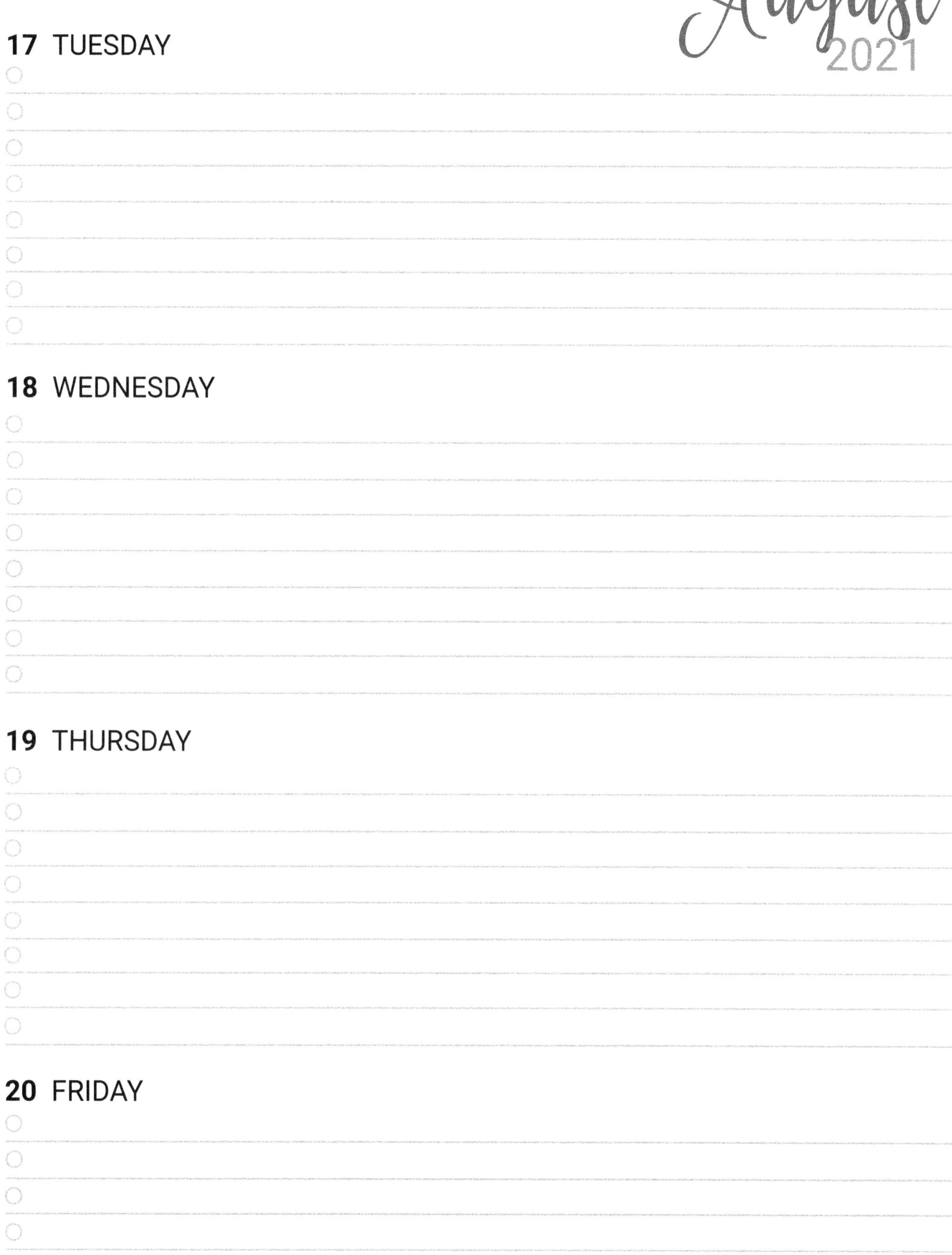
August
2021
17 TUESDAY
18 WEDNESDAY
19 THURSDAY
20 FRIDAY

August 2021

21 SATURDAY

22 SUNDAY

23 MONDAY

24 TUESDAY

25 WEDNESDAY

26 THURSDAY

27 FRIDAY

28 SATURDAY

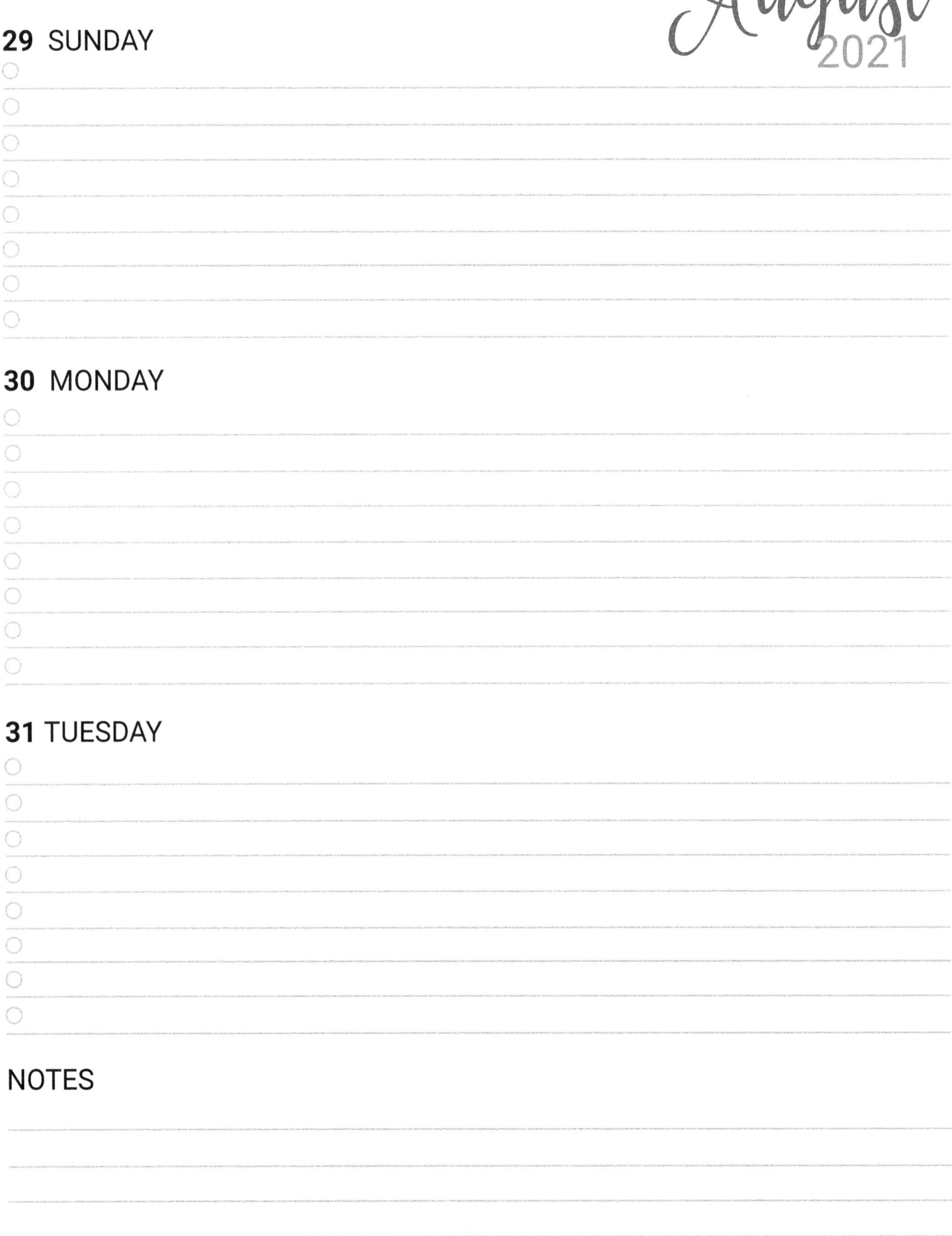

August
2021

29 SUNDAY

30 MONDAY

31 TUESDAY

NOTES

September
2021

01 WEDNESDAY

02 THURSDAY

03 FRIDAY

04 SATURDAY

September
2021

05 SUNDAY

06 MONDAY

07 TUESDAY

08 WEDNESDAY

September
2021

09 THURSDAY

10 FRIDAY

11 SATURDAY

12 SUNDAY

September
2021

13 MONDAY

14 TUESDAY

15 WEDNESDAY

16 THURSDAY

September
2021

17 FRIDAY

18 SATURDAY

19 SUNDAY

20 MONDAY

September
2021

21 TUESDAY

22 WEDNESDAY

23 THURSDAY

24 FRIDAY

September
2021

25 SATURDAY

26 SUNDAY

27 MONDAY

28 TUESDAY

29 WEDNESDAY

30 THURSDAY

NOTES

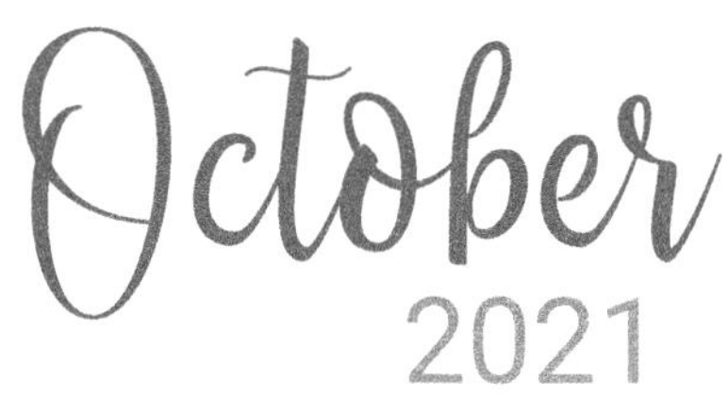

01 FRIDAY

02 SATURDAY

03 SUNDAY

04 MONDAY

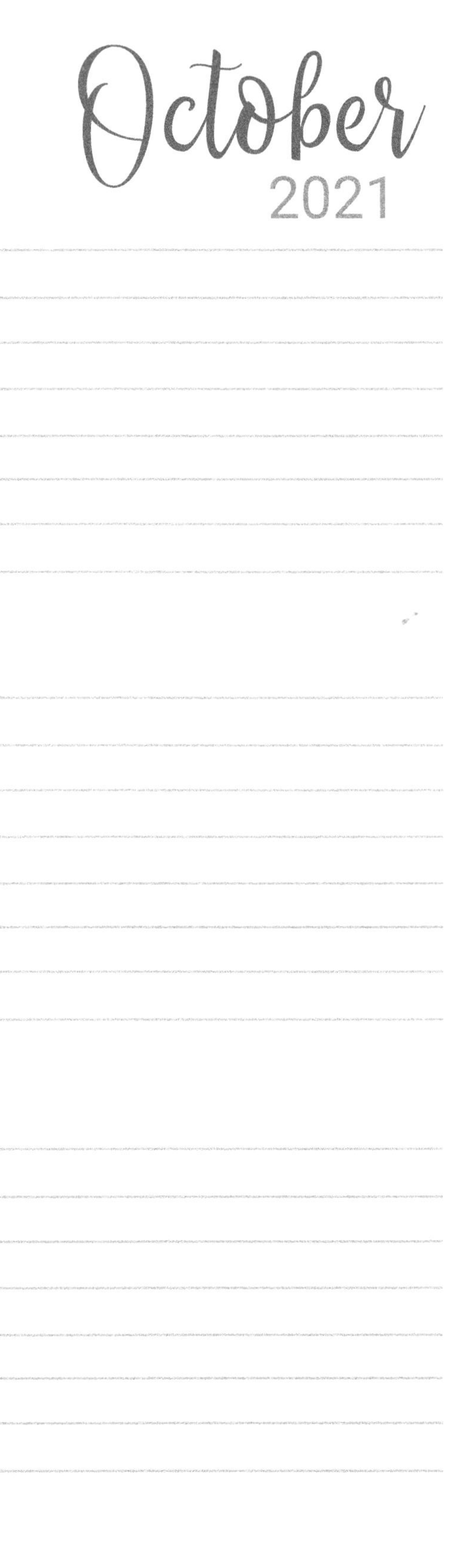

05 TUESDAY

06 WEDNESDAY

07 THURSDAY

08 FRIDAY

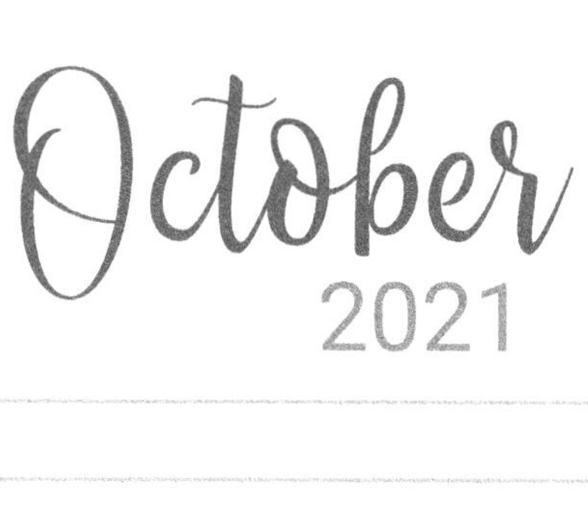

09 SATURDAY

10 SUNDAY

11 MONDAY

12 TUESDAY

13 WEDNESDAY

14 THURSDAY

15 FRIDAY

16 SATURDAY

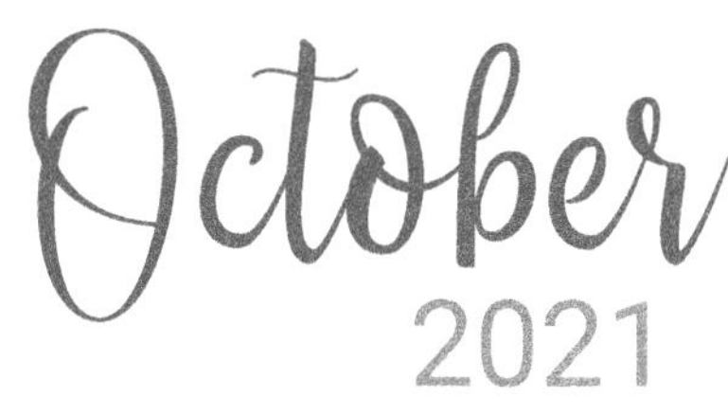

17 SUNDAY

18 MONDAY

19 TUESDAY

20 WEDNESDAY

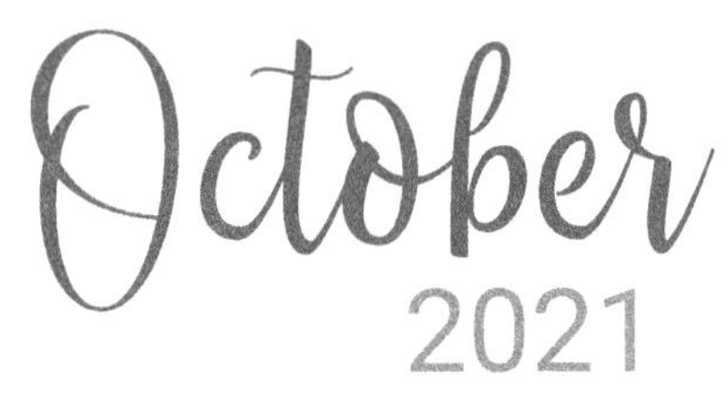

21 THURSDAY

22 FRIDAY

23 SATURDAY

24 SUNDAY

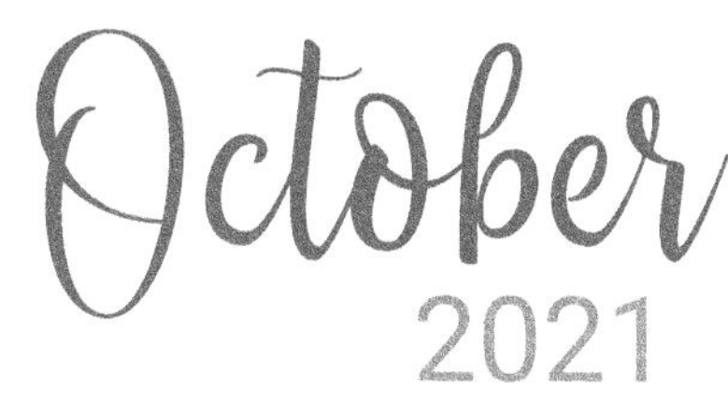

25 MONDAY

26 TUESDAY

27 WEDNESDAY

28 THURSDAY

October
2021

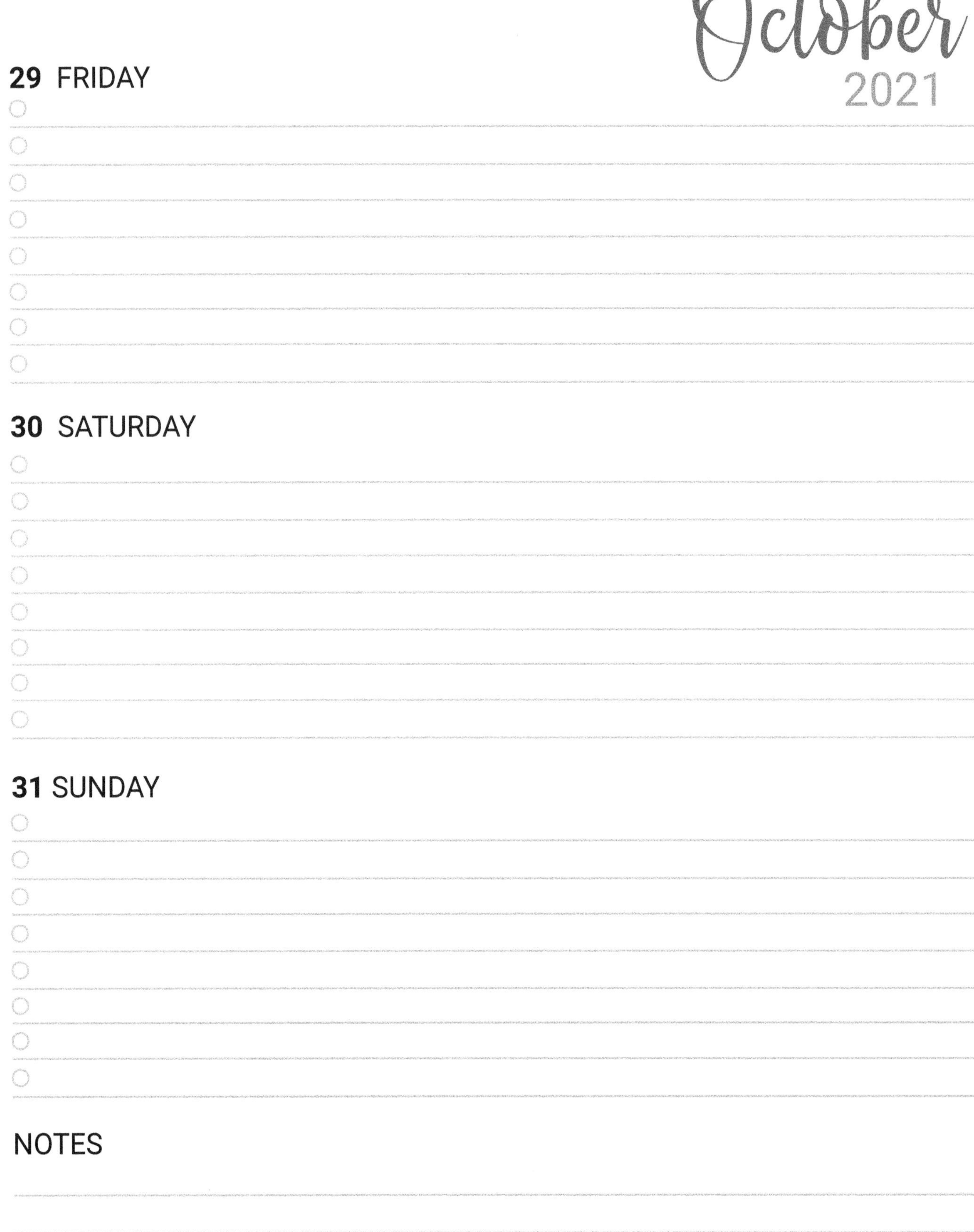

29 FRIDAY

30 SATURDAY

31 SUNDAY

NOTES

November
2021

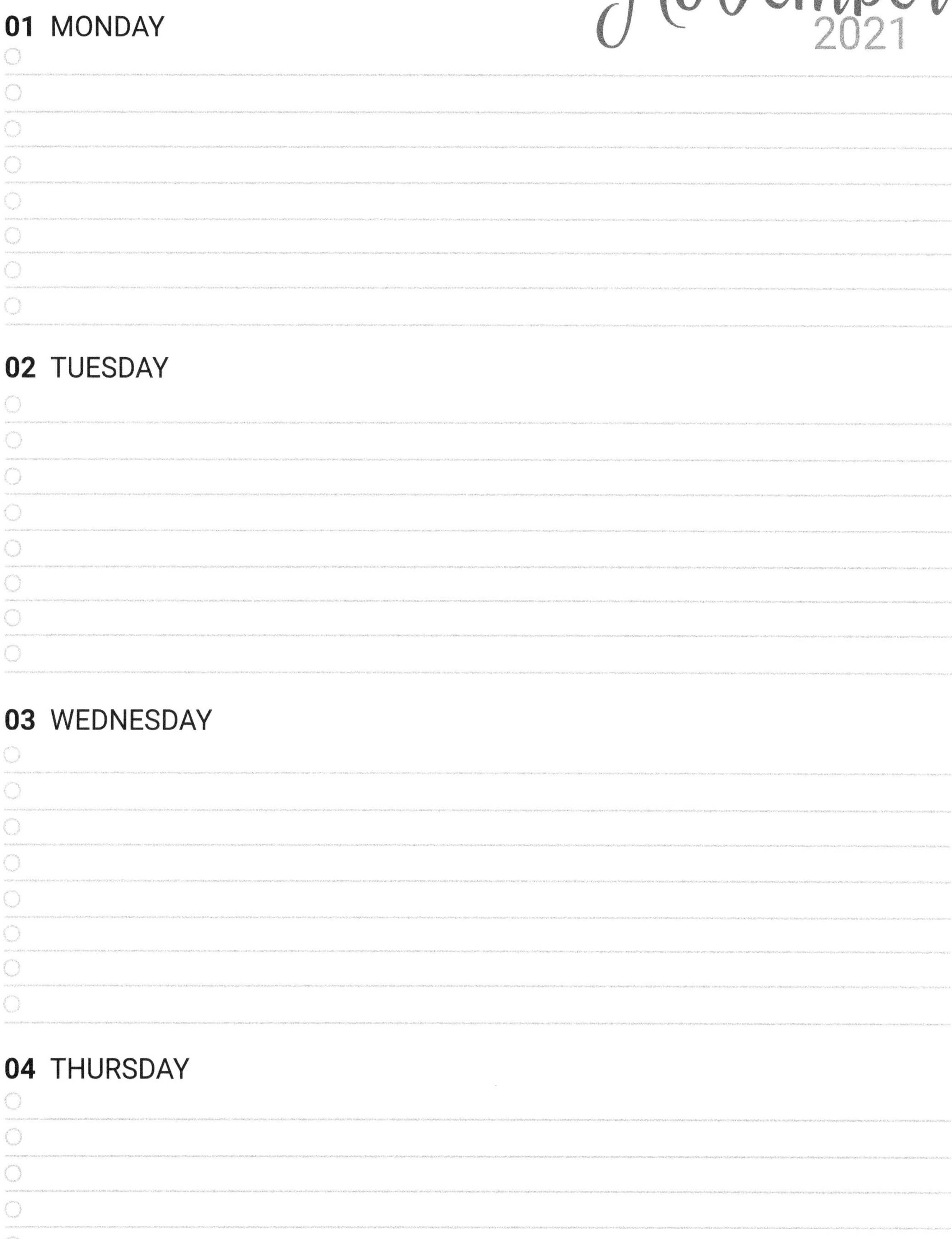

November
2021

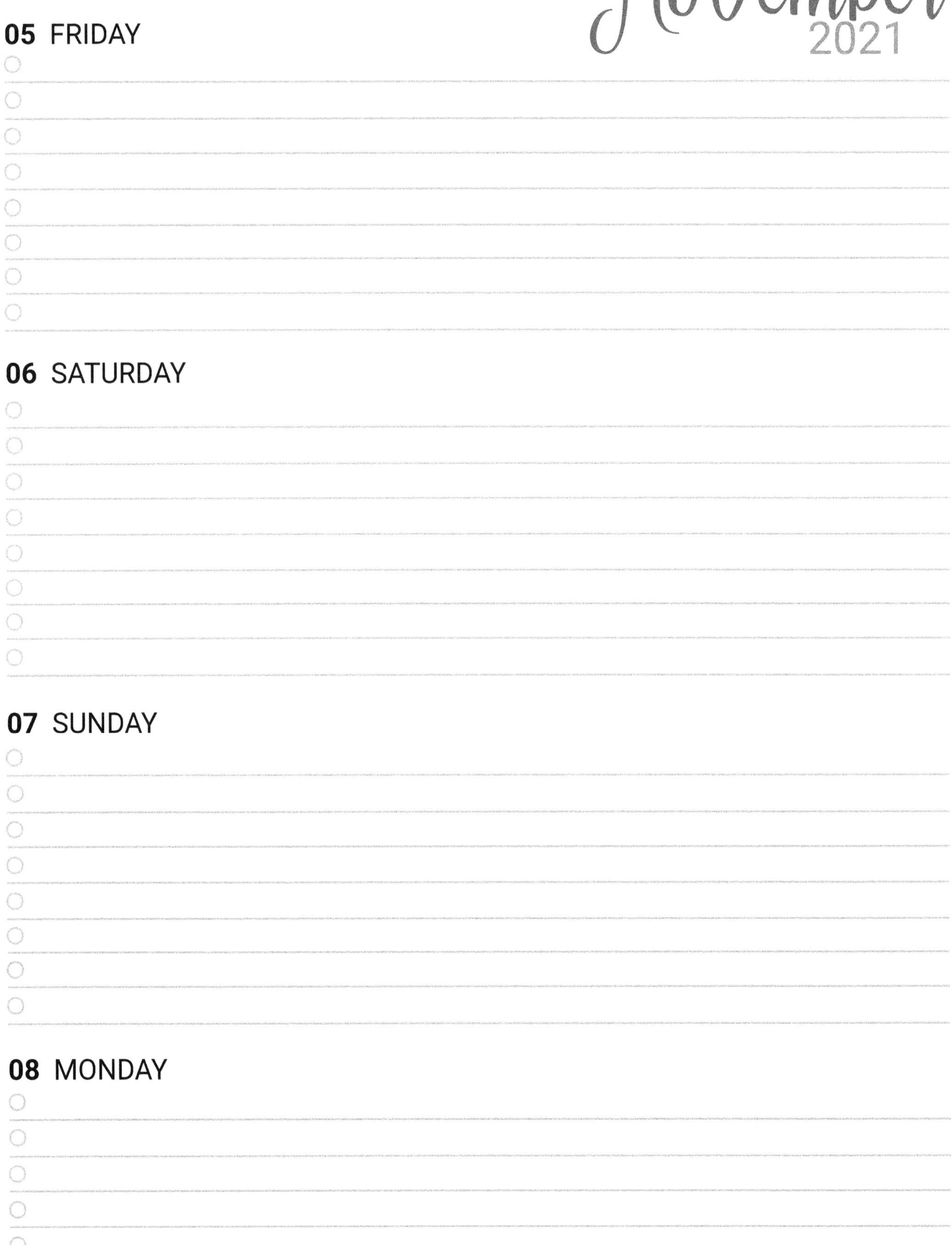

05 FRIDAY

06 SATURDAY

07 SUNDAY

08 MONDAY

November
2021

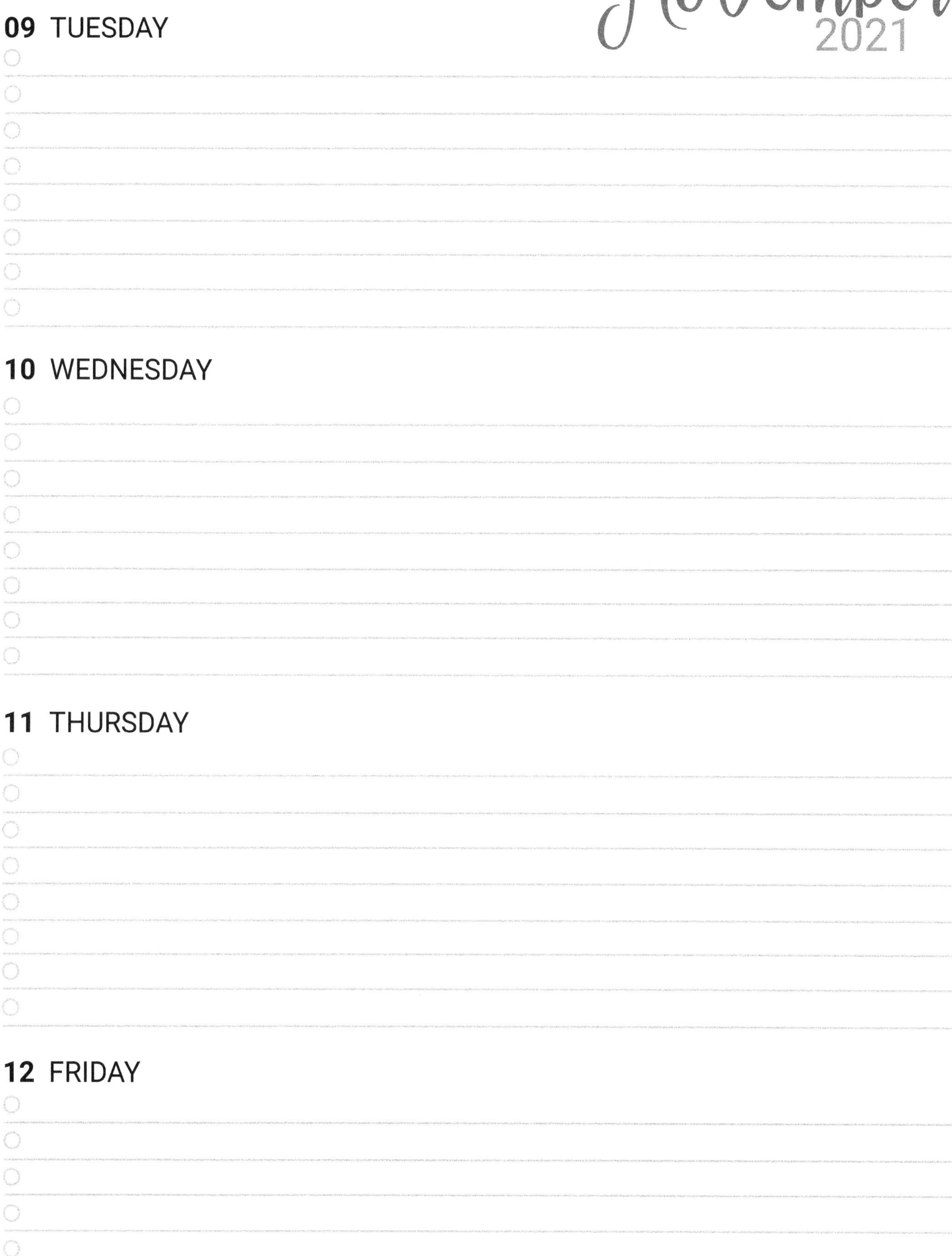

09 TUESDAY

10 WEDNESDAY

11 THURSDAY

12 FRIDAY

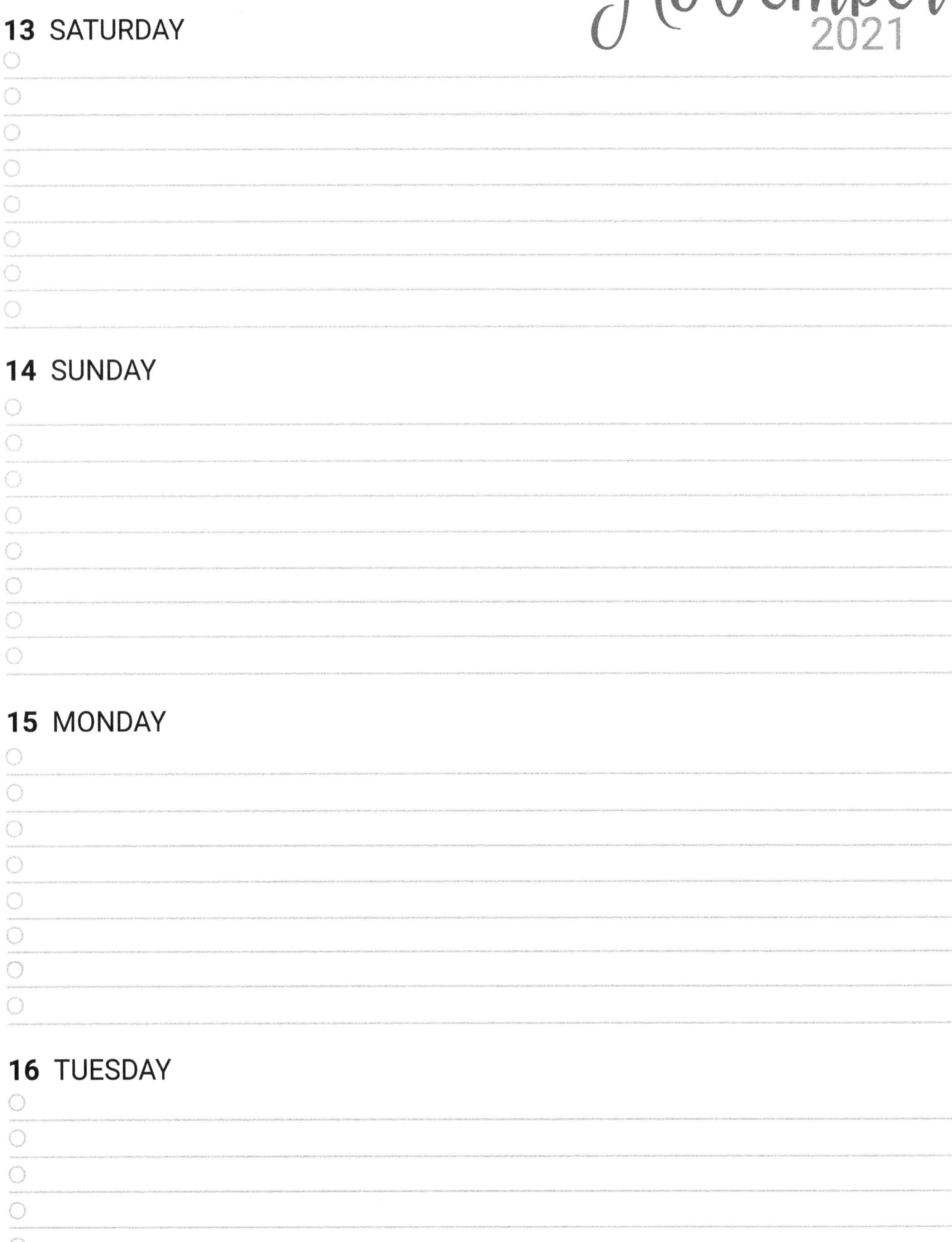
November
2021
13 SATURDAY
14 SUNDAY
15 MONDAY
16 TUESDAY

November 2021

17 WEDNESDAY

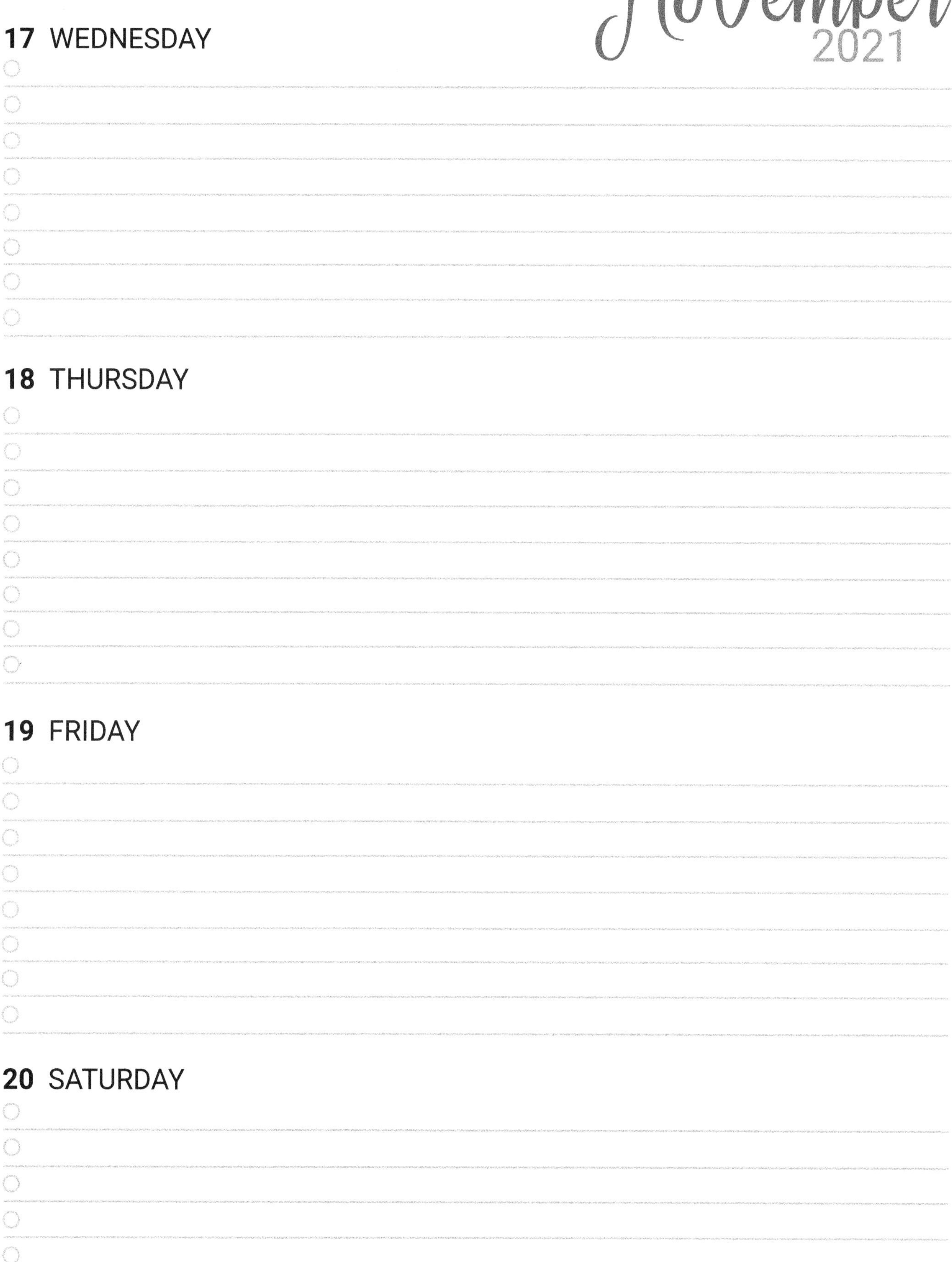

18 THURSDAY

19 FRIDAY

20 SATURDAY

November 2021

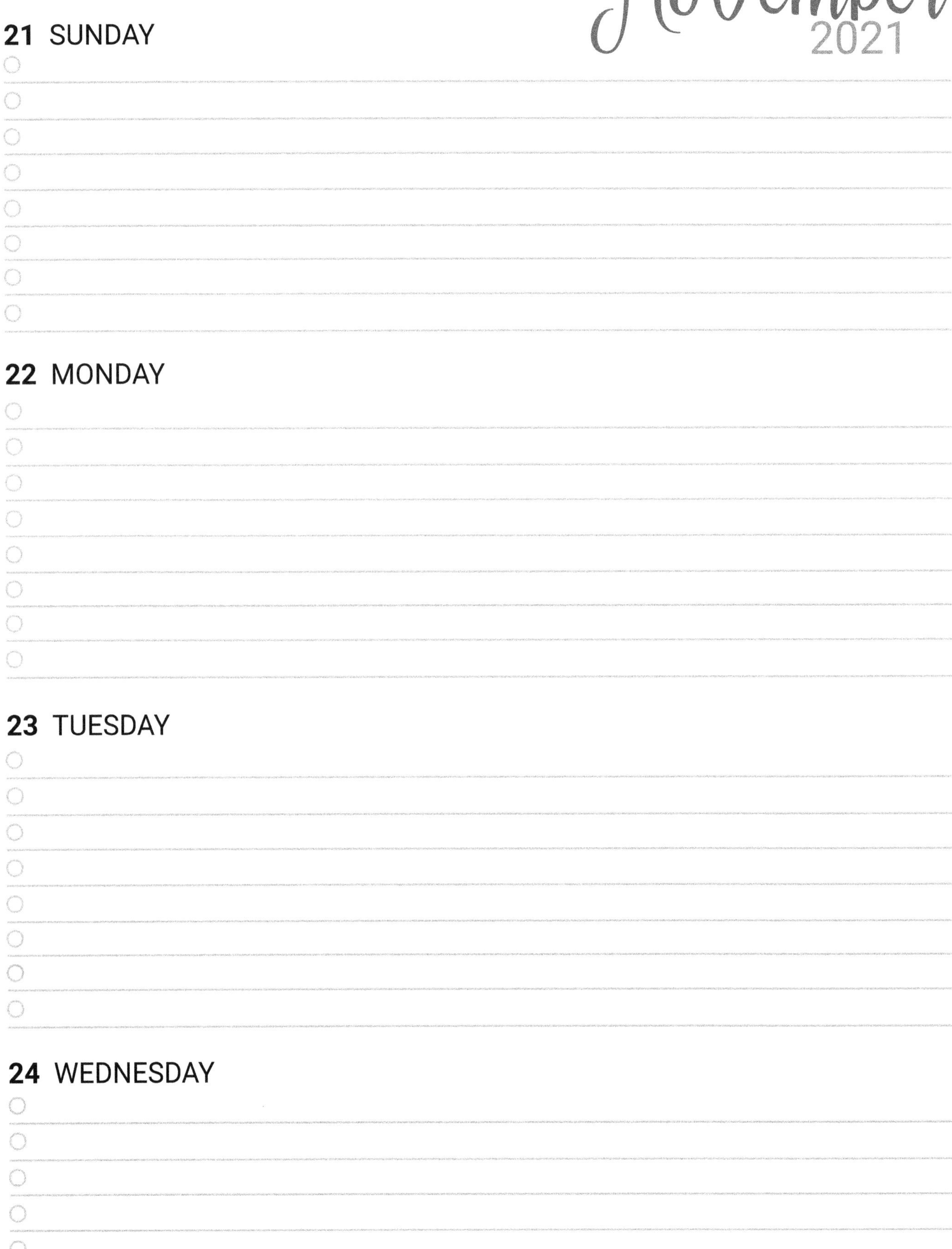

21 SUNDAY

22 MONDAY

23 TUESDAY

24 WEDNESDAY

November 2021

25 THURSDAY

26 FRIDAY

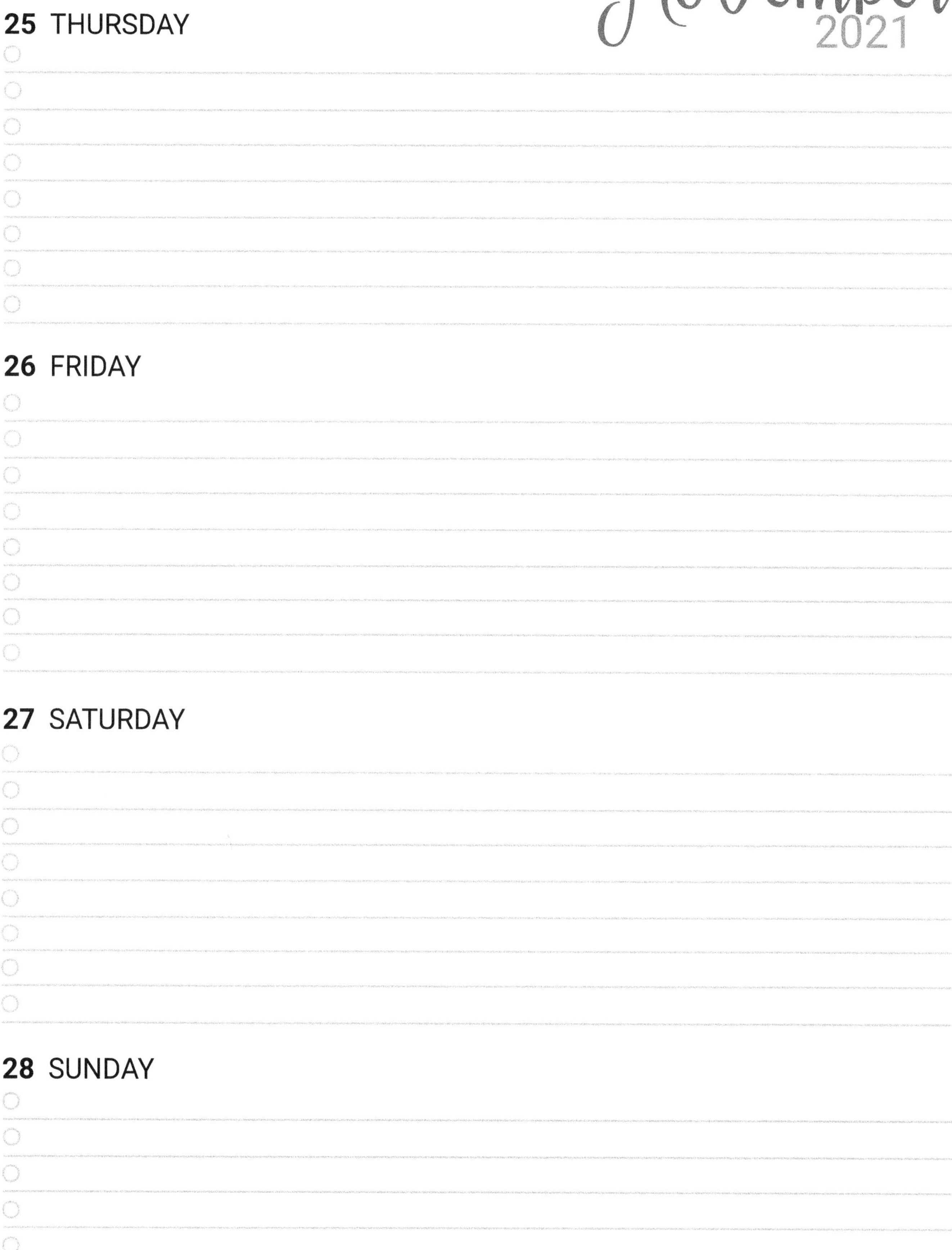

27 SATURDAY

28 SUNDAY

November 2021

29 MONDAY

30 TUESDAY

NOTES

December
2021

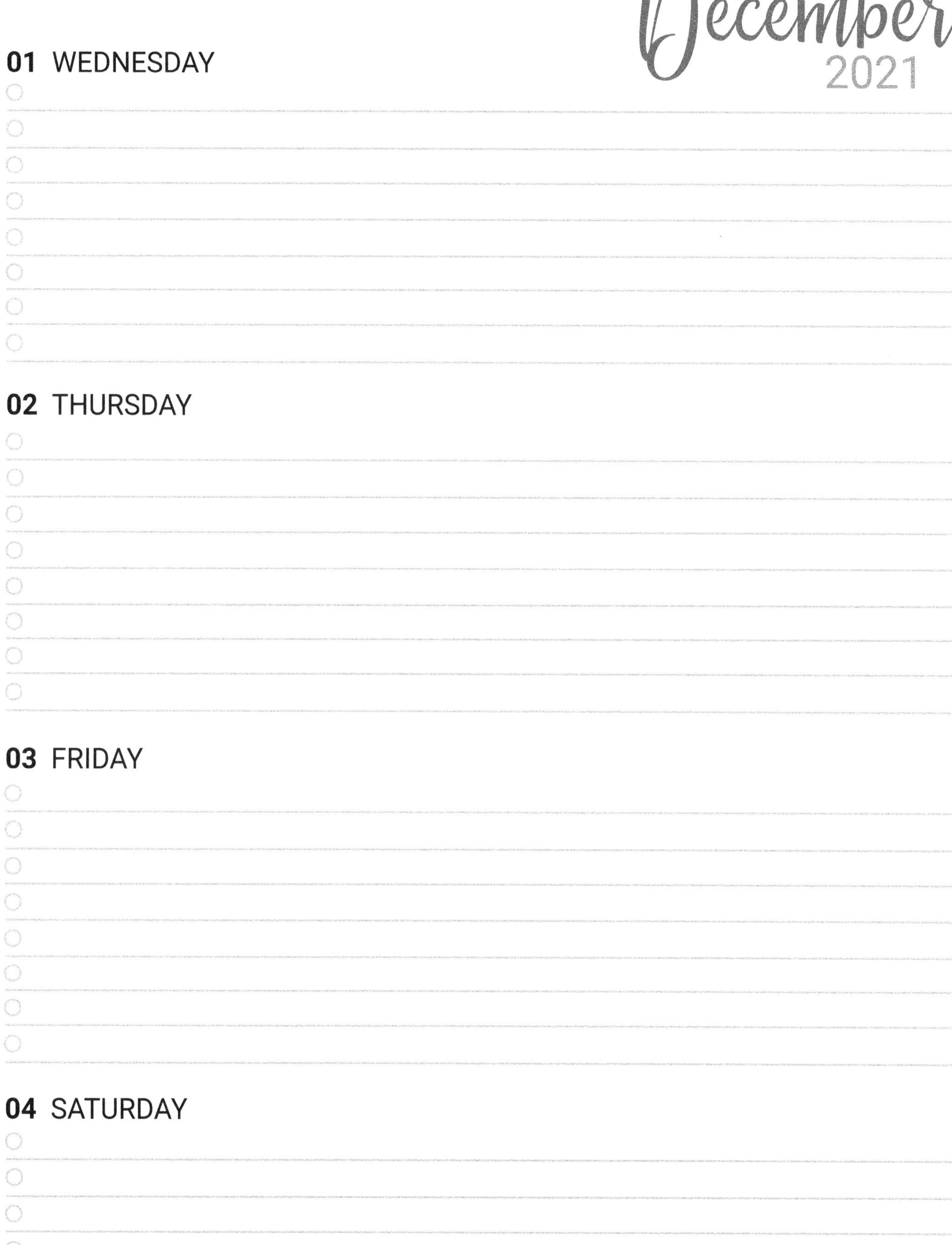

01 WEDNESDAY

02 THURSDAY

03 FRIDAY

04 SATURDAY

December
2021

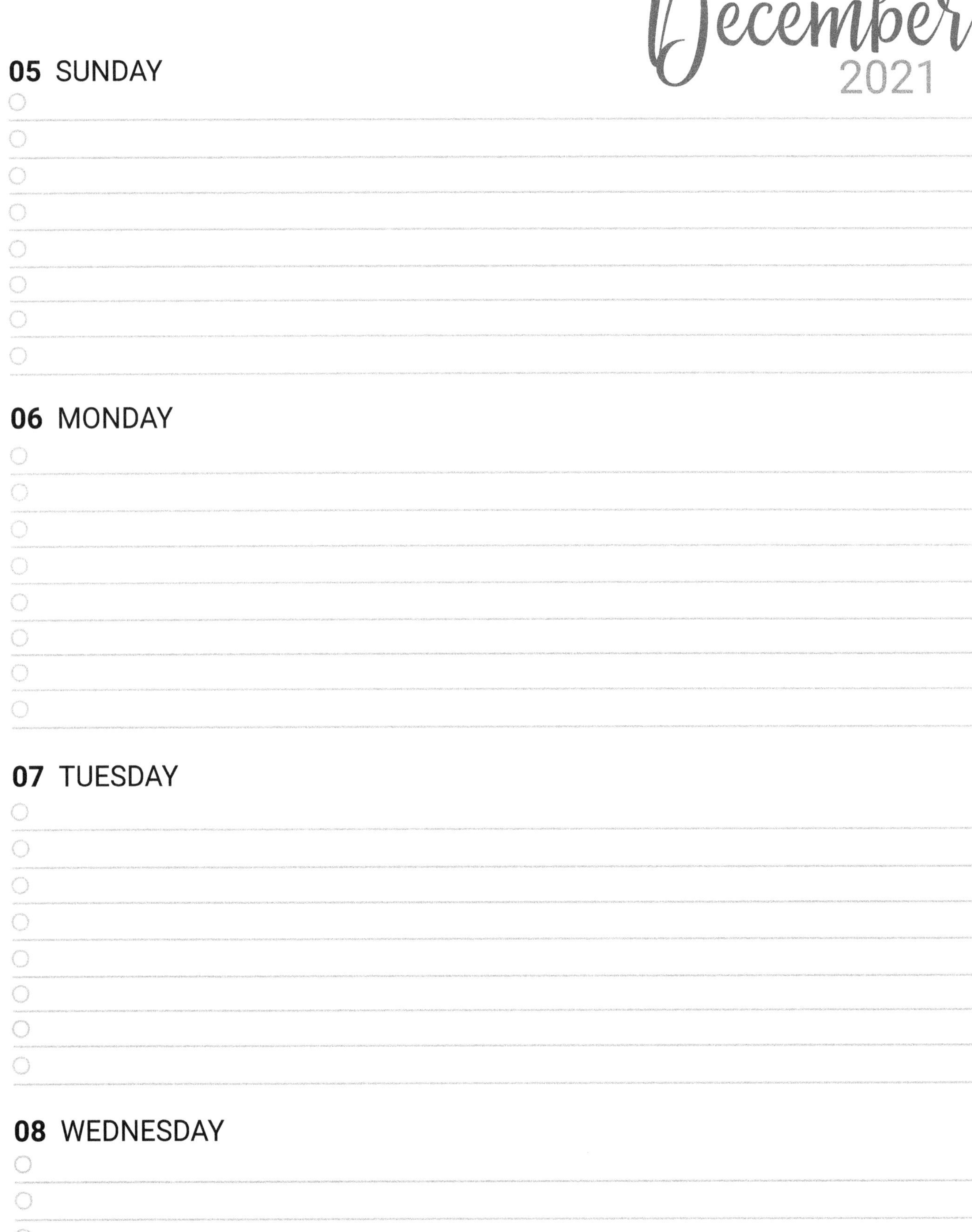

December
2021

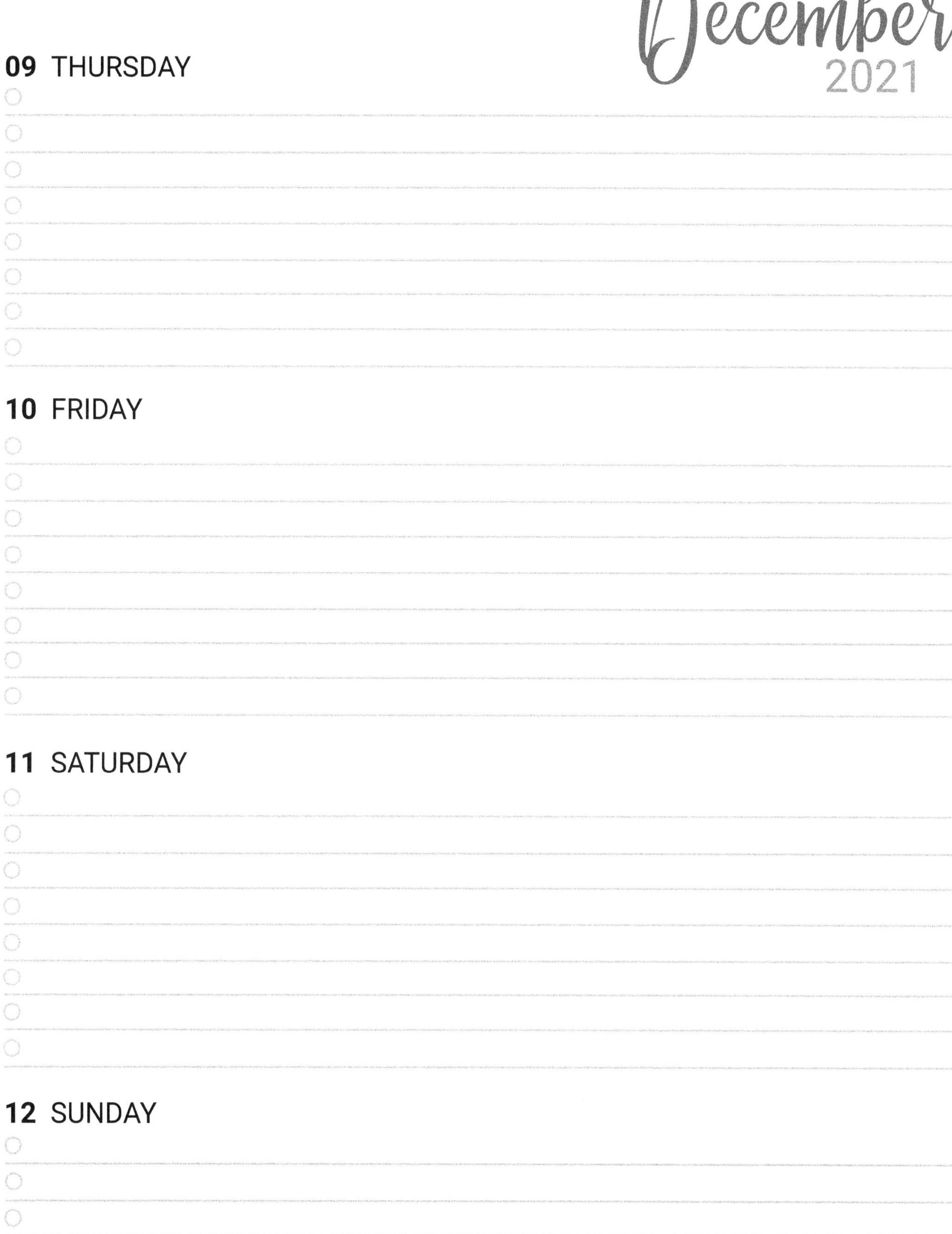

09 THURSDAY

10 FRIDAY

11 SATURDAY

12 SUNDAY

December
2021

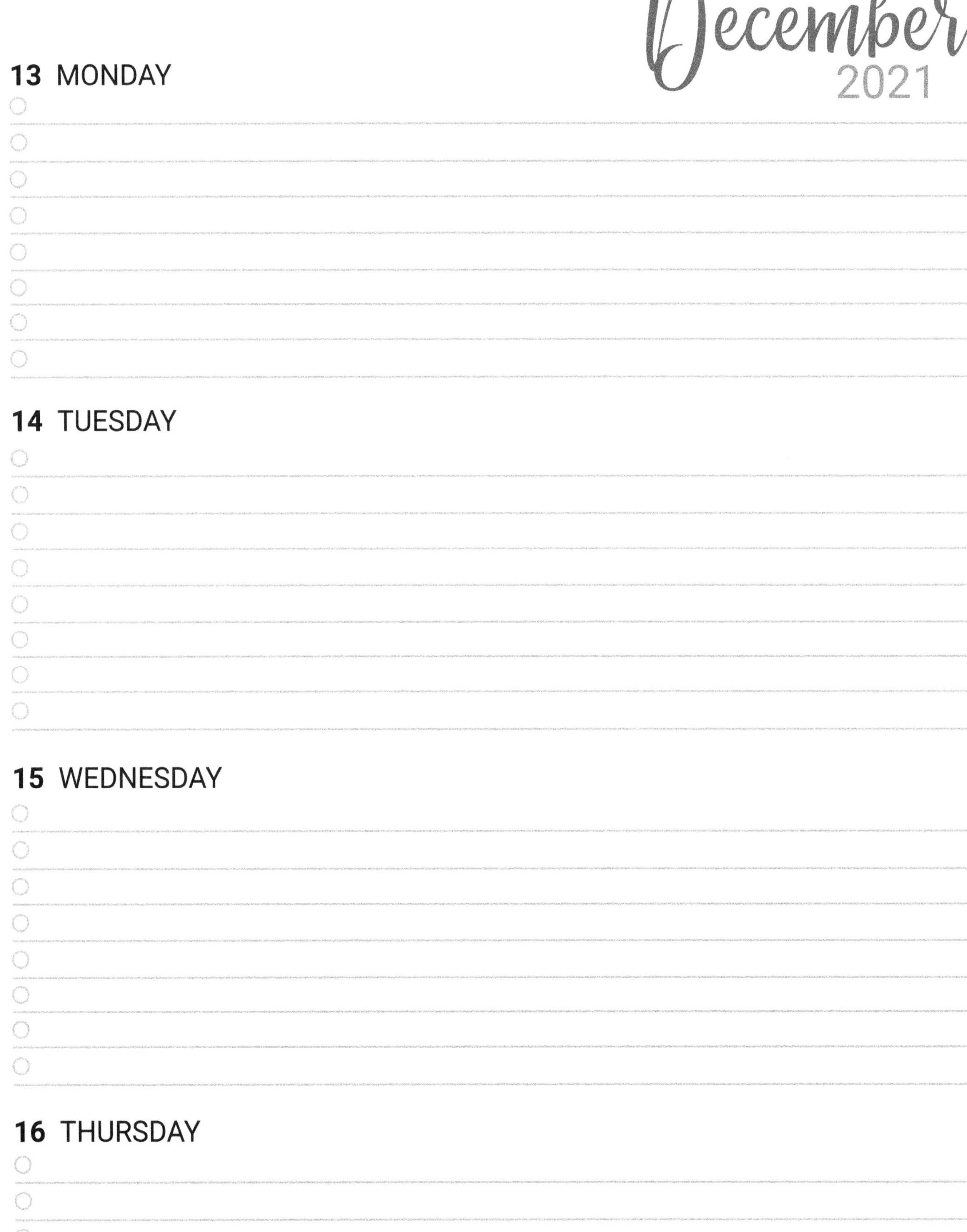

13 MONDAY

14 TUESDAY

15 WEDNESDAY

16 THURSDAY

December
2021

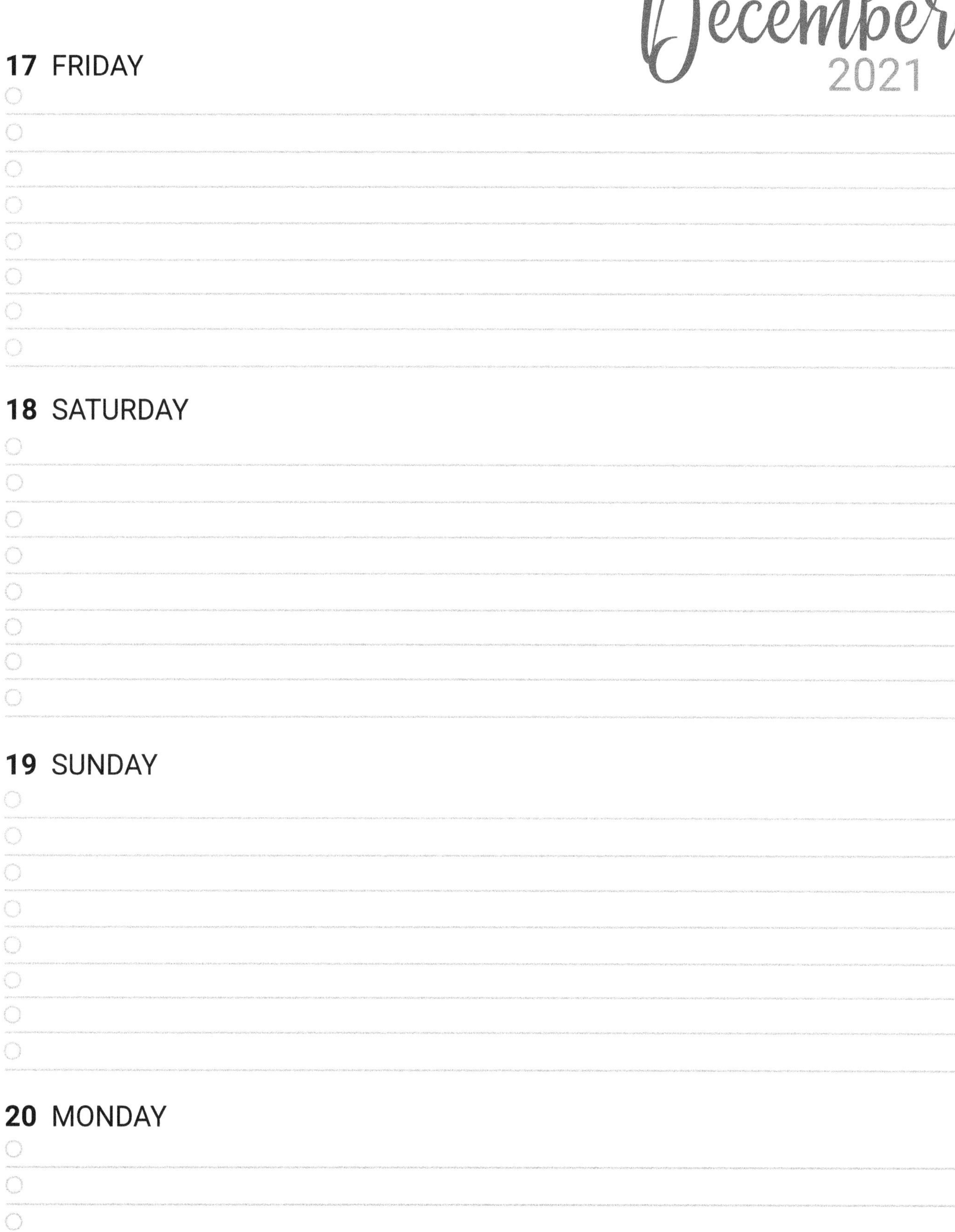

17 FRIDAY

18 SATURDAY

19 SUNDAY

20 MONDAY

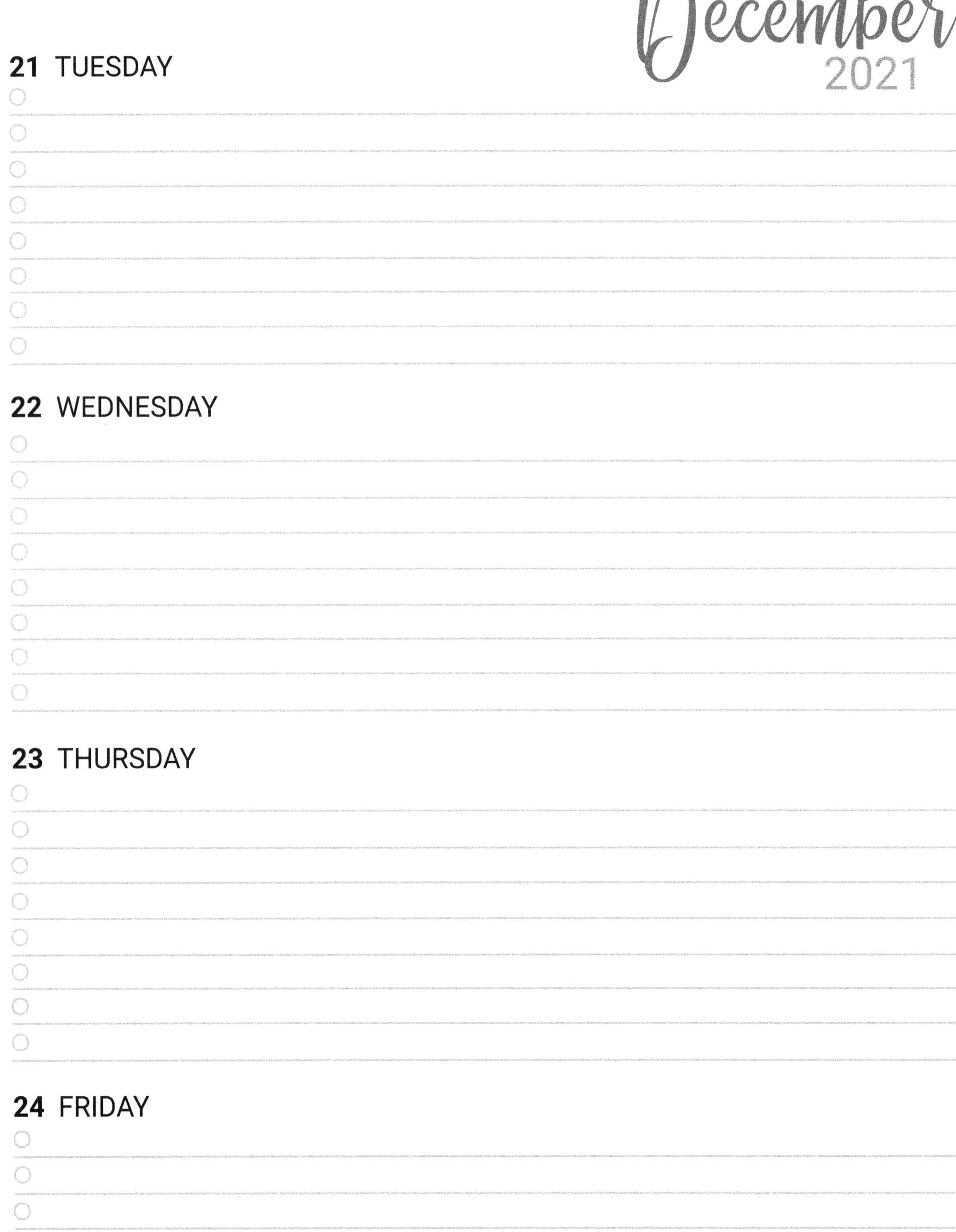

December
2021

21 TUESDAY

22 WEDNESDAY

23 THURSDAY

24 FRIDAY

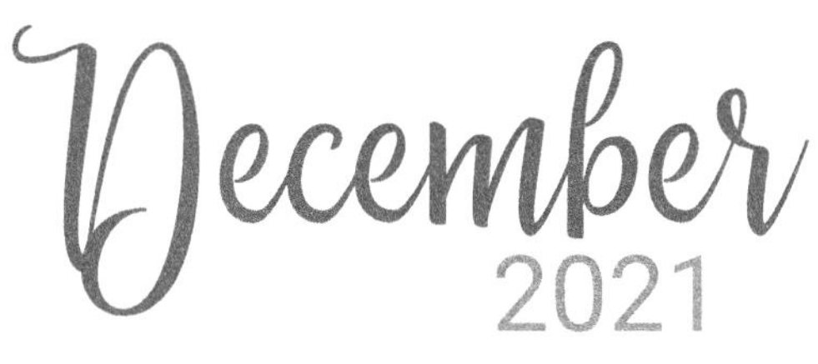

25 SATURDAY

26 SUNDAY

27 MONDAY

28 TUESDAY

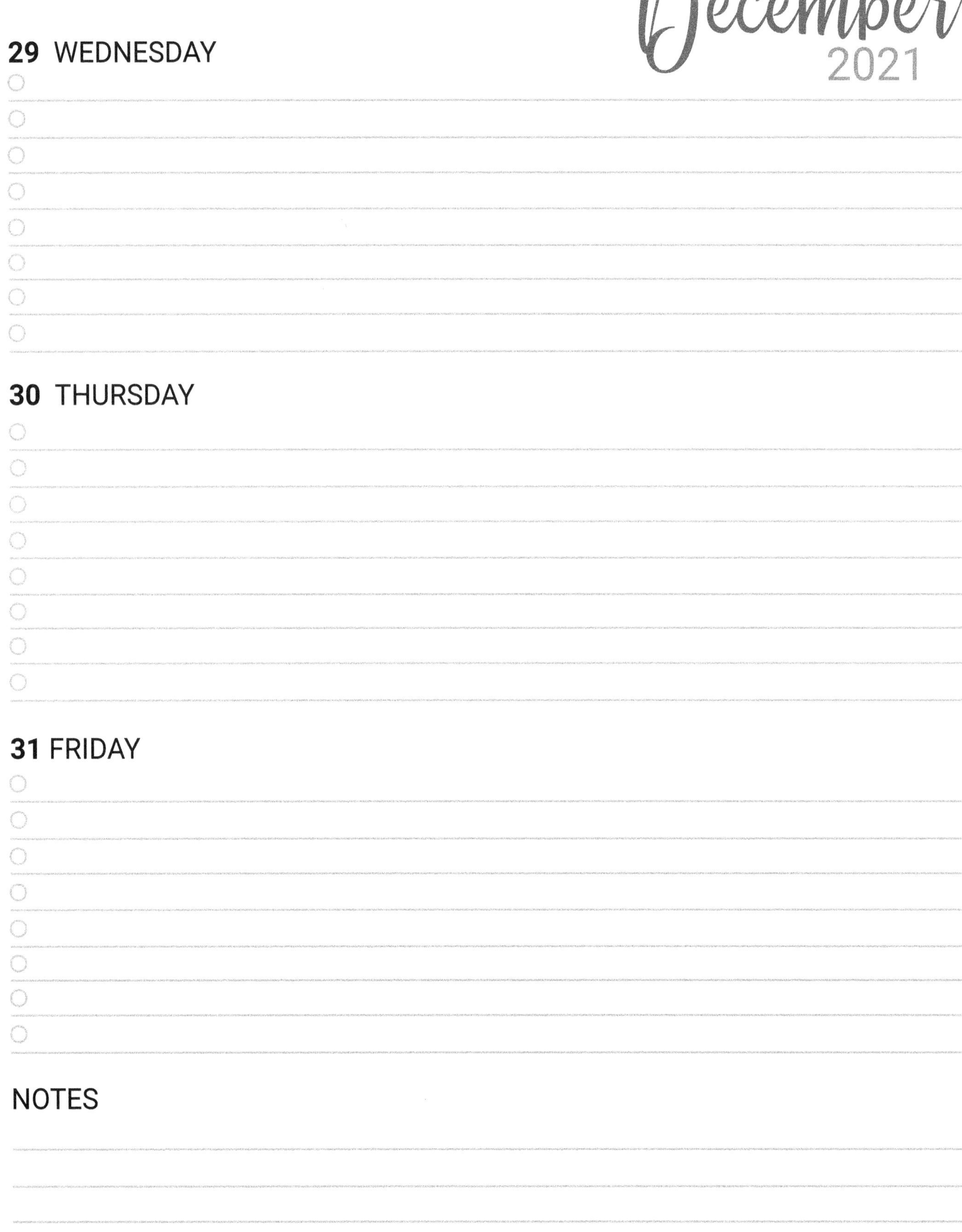

December 2021

29 WEDNESDAY

30 THURSDAY

31 FRIDAY

NOTES

www.ingramcontent.com/pod-product-compliance
Lightning Source LLC
Chambersburg PA
CBHW082147031125
34899CB00045B/1079

* 9 7 8 1 9 7 0 1 7 7 4 2 8 *